50 Cent

Other books in the People in the News series:

50 Cent

by Michael V. Uschan

LUCENT BOOKS
A part of Gale, Cengage Learning

GALE
CENGAGE Learning

Detroit • New York • San Francisco • New Haven, Conn • Waterville, Maine • London

© 2008 Gale, Cengage Learning

For more information, contact:
Lucent Books
27500 Drake Rd.
Farmington Hills, MI 48331-3535
Or you can visit our Internet site at gale.cengage.com

LIBRARY OF CONGRESS CATALOGING-IN-PUBLICATION DATA

Uschan, Michael V., 1948-
  50 cent / by Michael V. Uschan.
    p. cm. — (People in the news)
  Includes bibliographical references and index.
  ISBN 978-1-4205-0011-0 (hardcover)
  1. 50 Cent (Musician)—Juvenile literature. 2. Rap musicians—United States—Biography—Juvenile literature I. Title. II. Title: Fifty Cent.
  ML3930.A13U83 2007
  782.421649092—dc22
  [B]
                                                            2007030543

ISBN-10: 1-4205-0011-2

Printed in the United States of America
2 3 4 5 6 7 12 11 10 09 08

Contents

ame and celebrity are alluring. People are drawn to those who walk in fame's spotlight, whether they are known for great accomplishments or for notorious deeds. The lives of the famous pique public interest and attract attention, perhaps because their experiences seem in some ways so different from, yet in other ways so similar to, our own.

Newspapers, magazines, and television regularly capitalize on this fascination with celebrity by running profiles of famous people. For example, television programs such as *Entertainment Tonight* devote all their programming to stories about entertainment and entertainers. Magazines such as *People* fill their pages with stories of the private lives of famous people. Even newspapers, newsmagazines, and television news frequently delve into the lives of well-known personalities. Despite the number of articles and programs, few provide more than a superficial glimpse at their subjects.

Lucent's *People in the News* series offers young readers a deeper look into the lives of today's newsmakers, the influences that have shaped them, and the impact they have had in their fields of endeavor and on other people's lives. The subjects of the series hail from many disciplines and walks of life. They include authors, musicians, athletes, political leaders, entertainers, entrepreneurs, and others who have made a mark on modern life and who, in many cases, will continue to do so for years to come.

These biographies are more than factual chronicles. Each book emphasizes the contributions, accomplishments, or deeds that have brought fame or notoriety to the individual and shows how that person has influenced modern life. Authors portray their subjects in a realistic, unsentimental light. For example, Bill Gates—the cofounder and chief executive officer of the software giant Microsoft—has been instrumental in making personal computers the most vital tool of the modern age. Few dispute his business savvy, his perseverance, or his technical expertise, yet critics say he is ruthless in his dealings with competitors and driven more by his desire to maintain Microsoft's dominance in the computer industry than by an interest in furthering technology.

In these books, young readers will encounter inspiring stories about real people who achieved success despite enormous obstacles. Oprah Winfrey—the most powerful, most watched, and wealthiest woman on television today—spent the first six years of her life in the care of her grandparents while her unwed mother sought work and a better life elsewhere. Her adolescence was colored by promiscuity, pregnancy at age fourteen, rape, and sexual abuse.

Each author documents and supports his or her work with an array of primary and secondary source quotations taken from diaries, letters, speeches, and interviews. All quotes are footnoted to show readers exactly how and where biographers derive their information and provide guidance for further research. The quotations enliven the text by giving readers eyewitness views of the life and accomplishments of each person covered in the *People in the News* series.

In addition, each book in the series includes photographs, annotated bibliographies, timelines, and comprehensive indexes. For both the casual reader and the student researcher, the *People in the News* series offers insight into the lives of today's newsmakers—people who shape the way we live, work, and play in the modern age.

Worth a Lot More Than "Fifty Cents"

A t thirty years of age, very few people have achieved enough to justify writing their autobiography or starring in a movie about their life. Curtis James Jackson III, known by the world as the rapper 50 Cent, is one of those rare individuals. *From Pieces to Weight: Once Upon A Time in Southside Queens* was published on August 9, 2005, just one month after his 30th birthday. Three months later, on November 9, *Get Rich or Die Tryin'* opened in theaters across the nation. The movie was a fictionalized account of 50 Cent's life. In a review of the movie, film critic Roger Ebert complimented 50 Cent for doing a good job of acting. He claimed that the real star of the film was the dramatic story of the young rapper's life. Ebert wrote:

> The film is inspired by the haunting life story of Curtis (50 Cent) Jackson, who never knew his father, whose mother was a drug dealer killed when he was young, who sold drugs on the streets of New York City, and survived nine gunshot wounds to become one of the best-selling recording artists of modern times. It has been an amazing life, and he is only 30.[1]

Get Rich or Die Tryin' mixes the basic facts of 50 Cent's life with fictional situations that help to create a story of his rise from poverty and crime to wealth and musical stardom. However, anyone

Jackson's life—so far—is told in the book From Pieces to Weight: Once Upon a Time in Southside Queens.

who reads *From Pieces to Weight* will realize that 50 Cent has had enough dramatic real life events to serve as the plots for several movies. Many of those experiences were horrible, like the time he was nearly shot to death. As in any good movie, however, 50 Cent's real life story had a happy ending because his ability to rap helped him to overcome the obstacles of his childhood and youth. As 50 Cent notes in the epilogue to his autobiography, "I am truly blessed. And I remind myself every day that if I'm in a good space now, it's because I been in a bad space for so long before."[2]

Young Curtis Becomes an Orphan

Curtis Jackson was born on July 6, 1975, in South Jamaica, a poor African American neighborhood on the south side of Queens, a suburb of New York City. From the very beginning, Jackson's life mirrored the harsh poverty, danger, and destructive drug use that were a reality of life in South Jamaica and would later become the basis of some of his most powerful songs. Jackson never knew his father. His mother, Sabrina Jackson, was a drug addict. She raised him as a single parent, which was the norm in South Jamaica. "In my neighborhood, if you had both parents, you were spoiled," Jackson once claimed.[3]

Sabrina sold cocaine and heroin to support her drug habit and her son. Her lifestyle was so unstable and dangerous that she usually had her son live with her own parents. When Curtis was eight years old, Sabrina was murdered. It is believed the slaying was connected with her drug dealing, but no one has ever been arrested. After his mother's death, Curtis lived full-time with his grandparents, Curtis and Beulah Jackson.

A Life of Drugs

The Jacksons loved their grandson and did their best to provide the orphaned boy with a normal family life. Curtis returned their love and even as an adult he continued to deeply respect his grandparents for everything they did for him. But like his mother before him, Curtis gave in to the temptations of making easy money by selling drugs. He began dealing drugs on a street corner in his neighborhood when he was twelve years old and dropped out of school after the tenth grade to sell drugs full-time. He was eventually arrested several times in 1994 and was sentenced to seven months in a youth correctional program. When Jackson was freed, he began selling drugs again even though he knew he could be killed like his mother, or put in prison if he was caught once more. But the drug trade was the only way an uneducated youth like Jackson could make much money. In 1997, Jackson's son, Marquise, was born. He decided then to find another way to make a living because he did not want his son to grow up as he had—without a parent.

Curtis Becomes 50 Cent

Like many young people in his neighborhood, Curtis liked rap music. He had even made up some songs and performed them for his friends. Many young blacks have tried to become rap stars as a way to escape the poverty and crime of the inner city. Under the nickname 50 Cent, Jackson was one of the few young blacks who would make that dream a reality. In only a few years, 50 Cent was recording best-selling rap albums like *The Massacre*, performing around the world, and starring in movies.

50 Cent's rise to fame and fortune was swift, but it was not easy. Just before 50 Cent hit the big time, he was shot nine times on May 24, 2000. His wounds hospitalized him for only a short time, but the shooting scared executives at Capital Records, and the company dropped him as a performer. After persevering for several years, 50 Cent was signed by another company and began making hit records that led to stardom. Said 50 Cent: "At one point, I was the only one who believed I was good. For a LONG period of time. My grandparents, I love them to death, but even they thought I was a little off."[4]

Curtis Jackson, better known as 50 Cent, had a book and a movie about his life before he was 31.

50 Billion?

Nobody thinks 50 Cent is crazy any more. By 2007, he had sold more than 20 million records to become the world's richest and most famous rapper. His 2005 income was estimated by *Forbes* magazine at $41 million, and 50 Cent—whose nickname can also mean a half-dollar—thinks he can earn much, much more. 50 Cent has told one magazine that "I feel like I could make a billion dollars easy."[5] That amount of money would be two billion 50-cent pieces.

Chapter 1

Growing Up Poor, Black, and an Orphan

5O Cent gave a series of interviews to reporters in the months before *Get Rich or Die Tryin'* opened in movie theaters on November 9, 2005. Some of these media sessions took place in 50 Cent's luxurious trailer on the set of the movie, which was filmed in Toronto, Canada. As one reporter was questioning 50 Cent, he noticed that the rapper was missing the top of one knuckle on his left hand. "That's from when I got shot," 50 Cent told him.[6]

The disfigurement of his hand was one of several injuries the rapper suffered in the shooting on May 24, 2000, that nearly took his life. Even today, the missing knuckle is a daily physical reminder of the harsh, dangerous life that 50 Cent led before he vaulted to fame and fortune as a rapper.

"Boo-Boo" Becomes an Orphan

50 Cent was born on July 6, 1975, in South Jamaica, a black inner city neighborhood in Queens, New York. Sabrina Jackson named her son Curtis James Jackson III after her father. Curtis and Beulah Jackson, her parents, had moved there years earlier from Ackerson, South Carolina. They had raised nine children, including one son who they named Curtis Jackson, Jr., which is why Sabrina's son became Jackson III.

The rap star grew up in South Jamaica, a poor black neighborhood in Queens, New York.

Curtis never knew his father. When the boy was old enough to ask where his dad was, his mother simply told him he did not have one. Sabrina was 15 years old when Curtis was born. His mother was a drug addict who supported herself by selling drugs. Although Sabrina loved Curtis—she affectionately nicknamed him "Boo-Boo"—she only saw him occasionally; he usually lived with her parents because her lifestyle was chaotic and dangerous.

Sabrina Jackson

Sabrina lavished gifts on Curtis when she would visit him or keep him overnight. Said 50 Cent: "She used to substitute finances [money] for time. Every time I seen her, it was somethin' new for me. Christmas every day. She put jewelry on me early."[7] Although Sabrina gave him love as well as presents, 50 Cent remembers that his mother could be aggressive and hard. He said, "She was really manly, she was really tough, and she had to be—she was hustling."[8] Curtis learned about this other side of his mother's personality by watching her sell drugs and how she interacted with other dealers.

At the time it was rare for a woman to sell drugs, and his mother undoubtedly needed a hard attitude to make sure she was treated fairly by the people she dealt with. But her tough exterior could not protect her from the violence that is common in the drug world. Sabrina was murdered when Curtis was eight years old. She died in her apartment after inhaling natural gas from a stove. Police said someone had killed her by spiking her drink to make her unconscious and then turned on the gas, closed the windows, and left.

Curtis's grandparents now had to raise him. They tried to turn the young boy away from drugs and the life of crime that had claimed their daughter, but they would fail.

A Teenage Drug Dealer

The Jackson home was crowded because eight of their children still lived there. Beulah Jackson lavished love on Curtis, but his older uncles and aunts often ignored him. Money was tight in the Jackson household. Curtis missed the presents his mother used to give him, and in a few years he began selling crack cocaine and heroin to get clothes, athletic shoes, and other things he wanted. It was easy for the young boy to get started in the drug trade because neighborhood dealers had known his mother. 50 Cent once explained in an interview how they helped him to start selling drugs:

Why 50 Cent Started Selling Drugs

Curtis James Jackson III followed in his mother's footsteps and started selling drugs because it was the only way he could get money to buy clothes and other things he wanted. He once said:

> When you grow up without finances [money] it starts to feel like finances are the answers to all your problems. And when you're like twelve years old and you're having a hard time in school and they're telling you, "You can do well in school for eight more years and have the things you want," a kid's curiosity leads him to the 'hood. And he finds someone who got it [money] and didn't go to school. They [drug dealers] persuade you, they tell you, "No, you can get paid like *this*.' You go off into a whole other zone, it's, "This is how I gotta do." And even if you're only generating enough finances to purchase a vehicle, you're still taking care of yourself better than your people can.

Ethan Brown, *Queens Reigns Supreme: Fat Cat, 50 Cent, and the Rise of the Hip-Hop Hustler*. New York: Anchor Books, 2005, p. 140.

I started hustling at twelve; my mother hustled ahead of me. I was only allowed to because they [drug dealers] knew me, "Oh, that's Sabrina's little boy. Let him do something." In that situation I felt like I had no option [to get money any other way].[9]

A Secret Life

Curtis kept his drug dealing secret because he loved his grandmother and did not want to hurt her. He sold drugs on Guy

A Lonely Little Boy

When 50 Cent was growing up, he lived with his grandparents and their eight children. His many uncles and aunts were older than he was and would often tell him to go away because he was bothering them. In *From Pieces to Weight: Once Upon A Time in Southside Queens*, 50 Cent explains what he did when that happened:

> I was always a nosy kid, and as a reward for my inquisitiveness, I would be quickly banished from the vicinity of anything worth eavesdropping on: "Stay outta grown folks business. Go upstairs." I was always the little [boy] upstairs. I got to know the upstairs real well—me and my little green army men. I used to talk to them like they were real people. "They always making me go upstairs," I'd say. And my army men would reply, "That's cause they're stupid. They're not as smart as we are. We could have more fun without them." "You know what. I think you're right."

50 Cent with Kris Ex, *From Pieces to Weight: Once Upon A Time in Southside Queens*. New York: MTV Books, 2005, p. 10.

R. Brewer Boulevard after school from 3 P.M. to 6 P.M. and on weekends. To explain his absence on weekdays, he claimed he was in an after-school program. That lie was only one of the ways in which Curtis concealed his drug dealing. He also learned to develop two distinctly different personalities—the hard, tough guy on the street who sold drugs, and the gentle, obedient young boy at home who loved his grandmother. This is how 50 Cent explained the split personality he developed to thrive in both worlds: "Me, I had to be two people: I had to be aggressive enough to get by in the neighborhood and then my grandma's baby in the house."[10]

Curtis worked hard at his trade and was soon making enough money to buy the things he wanted. In his autobiography, 50 Cent wrote that:

The more I did it, the easier it got. And the easier it got, the more of *it* [money] I got. At first, I was able to do small things like buy snacks and fast food. Then I was able to get sneakers and clothes. Then I started getting little handheld video games, but that didn't make sense. I didn't have time to play any games; I was too busy selling coke.[11]

Curtis Gets Busted at School

Curtis was so good at selling drugs that after a few years he was able to buy a car. He hid the car from his grandparents by keeping it at a friend's home and riding there and back on his bicycle. He also bought a gun. Although 50 Cent has never said much about the shootings he was involved with, he claims in his autobiography that he shot people several times when they tried to rob or attack him. Curtis was also able to defend himself on the street with his fists. When he was fourteen years old, Curtis started boxing at a gym that was set up by a drug dealer. Although he quickly learned boxing techniques, 50 Cent claims he became a good fighter because he was able to control his anger.

School became boring for Curtis because he was making so much money dealing drugs. By the 10th grade, he was skipping class most of the time—he usually only went to school to show off new clothes. One of his infrequent visits to Andrew Jackson High School led to his first arrest. Curtis had always been careful not to take a gun, knife, or drugs to school because security guards searched students thoroughly when they entered the building. But one day a guard found some cocaine that Curtis had accidentally left in an athletic shoe in his book bag.

School officials called police and Curtis was arrested and charged with possession of a controlled substance. The school suspended

Eight Facts about "Fitty"

Fact 1: His real name is Curtis James Jackson III

Fact 2: He named himself "50 Cent" after Kelvin Martin, a deceased New York gangster.

Fact 3: His mentor was Jason William Mizell, better known as Jam-Master Jay of Run-D.M.C.

Fact 4: He has his own successful clothing and shoe line called G-Unit.

Fact 5: He purchased the former mansion of ex-boxer Mike Tyson for a reported $4.1 million.

Fact 6: He has earned 11 Grammy nominations.

Fact 7: He wanted to be a boxer when he was a teenager.

Fact 8: He has a son, Marquise, who is sometimes called "25 Cent."

him for two weeks. The punishment did not bother Curtis, but having to explain what had happened to his grandmother did upset him.

Learning the Truth

When Curtis told his grandmother about being caught with drugs at school, she had a revelation of her own for him. For the first time, she explained to her grandson how his mother had died. Until then, his grandparents had told him that his mother had died in her sleep. Curtis realized they had been trying to protect him by keeping the details from him. But at the same time, Curtis also realized something else: "In a way, I was my mother's son. Seeing [learning about] her getting money from hustling at a young age definitely altered me."[12]

Curtis was upset about hurting his grandmother. But once she knew the truth, it was easier for him to sell drugs because he no longer had to hide his activities at home. Curtis' uncles and aunts used drugs and drank heavily at home. In fact, when he was a small boy, they had often sent him out into the street to buy drugs for them.

More Trouble From Another Arrest

During his two-week suspension from school, Curtis sold drugs full-time. He continued dealing even after the courts placed him on probation for eighteen months for the drug charge. It was not long, however, before Curtis got into trouble again. Six months later, Curtis was talking to some friends selling drugs on a South Jamaica street when they were all arrested by undercover police officers. Curtis had just come from a meeting with his probation officer. He was not carrying drugs and had not been doing anything illegal. But when Curtis was arrested with the others, officials reviewed his probation records. Even though Curtis did not use drugs, he had tested positive for cocaine in a court-mandated urine test; he was handling so much cocaine that residue from the drugs on his hand had seeped into his blood system. Believing that Curtis needed help for a drug problem, the court sentenced him to twenty-two months in a drug rehabilitation program.

Curtis had to live with other juveniles in a dormitory-style apartment building in Brooklyn, New York. The program was an alternative to going to a juvenile institution or prison for young drug offenders. The program used counseling, supervised living, and group sessions to help young men and women quit using drugs. Curtis thought the treatment program was a joke but he went along with it because he did not want to go to jail. After several months, Curtis earned the right to "leave time," which meant he could be away from the group home for several hours each day. He used those hours to sell drugs, and when he was released, he went back to dealing full-time.

A Six-Month Sentence

By the time Jackson was eighteen years old, he was often making thousands of dollars a day selling drugs, and he owned several vehicles. But Jackson's luck ran out on the night of June 29, 1994, when he and sixteen-year-old Taiesha Douse were arrested for selling crack on Guy R. Brewer Boulevard in Queens, New York. The two worked as a team. Customers would tell Jackson how many $5 vials of crack they wanted to buy and he would signal Douse, who was waiting nearby with the drugs. But one customer that night was Kathleen Kragel, an undercover Queens narcotics officer. She and other officers arrested Jackson and Douse, and they were charged with criminal sale of a controlled substance in the third degree.

Jackson's legal situation became even worse on July 19 when police searched his grandmother's home, where he still lived. Police seized heroin, crack cocaine, a starter gun, and $695 in cash. The raid resulted in additional drug charges and Jackson now faced a possible sentence of three to nine years in prison. However, the court offered him the option of serving a six-month sentence in the "Shock Incarceration Program" instead of going to prison. The program at a correctional facility in Beaver Dams, New York, combined intense physical training with educational classes and substance-abuse training. Jackson chose the shock program because he knew it would be easier than serving time in prison.

Shock Incarceration Program

The program was like a military boot camp, but Jackson was strong and in good shape. He could endure the 5 A.M. wake-up call and the marching and other physical activities involved in the program. Instructors bullied youths all day in an effort to teach them humility and to make them learn to follow orders and respect authority. Jackson found this difficult; he usually reacted violently when people failed to show him respect. But he put up with the abuse in the program because he did not want to go to prison. 50 Cent said:

I had to accept a drill sergeant screaming in my face. You can not accept him screaming in your face and go do three to nine years in jail, or you can let them say what they gonna say and do six months. It's an easy decision ... I turned it [his sentence] into something a little easier.[13]

Jackson, who had dropped out of high school after the 10th grade, used the class time at the facility to get his General Equivalency Degree. But the program failed to convince Jackson that his criminal way of life was wrong. When he was released, Jackson returned home and once again began selling drugs.

Jackson Hits the Streets Again

After he was released, Jackson had to continue reporting to officials in the AfterShock part of the program. But even that did not stop him from getting back into the drug trade. Within six months he had made enough money to buy a motorcycle and a Toyota Land Cruiser. He later moved up in luxury and purchased a Mercedes. Even though he had no driver's license, Jackson was able to buy these vehicles because he paid cash to dealers who did not care whether the sale was legal. His operation grew so big that soon Jackson was running his own crack house—a place where people could buy and use the drug.

Violence had always been a part of the drug world—Jackson's own mother's murder was proof of that. But after he returned from boot camp, the violence in the local drug scene seemed to have escalated. One night when Jackson came home to his grandmother's house, he was attacked in an attempted robbery. Just as Jackson got to the front door, his attackers shot at him from a cargo van parked in the street. He escaped by jumping off the porch and running to the backyard, where he had a gun stashed.

Incidents like this and his recurring brushes with the law began to make Jackson realize that dealing drugs, while profitable, was a risky way to make a living. He knew that almost everyone involved in the drug trade wound up either dead or in prison. "It was comin'," Jackson began to think to himself. "Long as you stay there [selling drugs], you don't beat the odds."[14]

It was then that Jackson began to think about doing something else with his life. Eventually, Jackson would decide that his future lay as a rapper and not as a drug dealer.

Chapter 2

Curtis Jackson Becomes 50 Cent

In the end, it was not fear of being killed or going to prison that led Curtis James Jackson III to stop selling drugs—it was the fact he was going to become a father. Jackson was driving through South Jamaica one day when he spotted Shaniqua Tompkins at a bus stop. Jackson stopped his Toyota Land Cruiser and introduced himself. He asked Tompkins for her telephone number and was surprised when she refused. He met her again at a pizza parlor, and this time he did get her number. They started dating, and she became his girlfriend.

A Child on the Way

When Tompkins became pregnant, she told Jackson that she feared his drug dealing would set a bad example for their child. Jackson had never felt guilty about selling drugs; it was an accepted way of life in the inner city. It was also the only way he believed a young, uneducated black man could make enough money to have the things he wanted. But Tompkins' concerns about his lifestyle made him remember how sad he had been to grow up without a father (and, except for a few years, without a mother). In his autobiography, Jackson wrote that his desire to be a good father to his child made him quit dealing drugs:

Tanisha [his nickame for Shaniqua] really made me think long and hard about myself. She said that she didn't like the idea of having to raise a kid by herself if I wound up in jail, or worse. That's when I started to think about doing something besides selling drugs. I had a kid coming and I didn't want to raise my son or daughter in that world. And more important, I wanted to be there to be part of my child's life.[15]

His son Marquise was born in 1997. By that time, Jackson was striving to become a rapper.

How Jackson Became 50 Cent

Even as a child, Jackson had always enjoyed rap music. He had rapped a little for fun with friends at parties and on the street. "I wrote rhymes too. I loved music, but I never saw a way to break into it," 50 Cent once said.[16] The dream of a drug dealer wanting to become a rapper was not as unrealistic as it sounds because of the close relationship that existed in many urban areas between criminals and entertainers. In *Queens Reigns Supreme: Fat Cat, 50 Cent, and the Rise of the Hip-Hop Hustler,* author Ethan Brown describes how drug dealers like Kenneth "Supreme" McGriff began in the 1980s to finance rappers. After McGriff had served a prison sentence for a drug conviction, he and Irv Gotti started Murder Inc. Records, which is now known as The Inc. Records. The record company gave a start to rappers like Ashanti and Ja Rule (Jeffrey Atkins). Brown claims it was easy for dealers and rappers to work together because they had similar backgrounds. Brown wrote that this connection was especially strong in Queens, New York:

Hip-hop and hustling [drugs] were worlds apart, but their denizens [people] shared the same neighborhoods and even the same blocks. During the [1980s], the [south Queens] area was home to hip-hop pioneers such as Run-D.M.C. and Def Jam founder Russell Simmons, as well as notorious kingpins such as 'Preme [McGriff].[17]

Gangsta Rap

This relationship was solidified even further in the early 1990s when "gangsta rap" became rap's most popular style. Gangsta rap glorified drug use and violence, and the heroes of many of its songs were dealers and other criminals. Would-be gangsta rappers with no (or minimal) criminal lifestyles began to associate with dealers and gang members to improve their "street cred"—the reputation for being tough and outside the law that they needed to present to their fans.

Jackson commented once on the link between the two groups: "Everybody who sold drugs in my 'hood [neighborhood], the older people, all [are] in the music business now. If they're not in the business, they're protecting somebody in the business."[18] This connection was also clear in the stage names many rappers used. Some borrowed names of drug dealers like Ronnie Bumps, a legendary heroin dealer in southeast Queens. Jackson called himself "50 Cent" after Kelvin Martin, a gangster from New York's Fort Green projects who specialized in brutal robberies. "He had passed [died], but he was still respected on the streets, so I wanted to keep his name alive," is the explanation Jackson gave for taking the robber's name.[19]

Unlike many would-be rappers, Jackson already had a lot of "street cred" because he had been a drug dealer. And his criminal connection helped him to meet someone who got him started on the road to rap stardom.

Jam Master Jay

In 1988, a few months after his son Marquise was born, Jackson was at a nightclub. Friends from the drug world introduced him to Jason William Mizell, who was better known as Jam Master Jay, the founder of Run-D.M.C., a pioneering rap group from Queens. Mizell took a liking to Jackson and became the mentor he needed to become successful. Jackson was good at writing lyrics but he did not know how to arrange them to make a song. It was Mizell who taught him how to blend lyrics and music into a song:

> I didn't have anything to show [Mizell]. But then he gave me a beat tape [music] and I wrote some rhymes to it. He loved

Jam Master Jay became the music mentor Jackson needed to become successful.

50 Cent and Jam Master Jay

50 Cent has always credited Jam Master Jay (Jason William Mizell) of the famed rap group Run-D.M.C. for helping him learn how to be a rapper. He explains some of the things Jam Master Jay taught him:

> A friend of mine introduced me to [him]. It's funny— I was in the street, hustling, and I made some relationships, some people that I met... like, they knew people in the music business and they introduced me to Jam Master Jay. It's weird who you know puts you on [gives you an opportunity], and what you know determines how long you stay once you get there. I didn't know how to write choruses, for example, and I learned that under him. Like, I had never been in a studio to record a record or make a demo or anything. That's the first time I was in a booth, in front of a mike, attempting to make a song was with Jam Master Jay. Everything—my song structure, counting bars—I learned from Jay. That was the first time I ever went to the studio and attempted to make a record for real.

Ethan Brown, *Queens Reigns Supreme: Fat Cat, 50 Cent, and the Rise of the Hip-Hop Hustler.* New York: Anchor Books, 2005, p. 30.

the rhymes, but some of them weren't right. One was too long, one was too short. He taught me how to count bars, the song structure, all that comes from Jam Master Jay.[20]

A Record Contract

Mizell also helped Jackson to get started professionally. Jackson's first recording appearance was in 1998 on "React," one of the songs in the album *Shut 'Em Down* by Onyx. In 1999, Jam Master helped Jackson—who was now calling himself 50 Cent—get his first record contract. 50 Cent signed with Columbia Records through the Track Masters label, which had already featured famous singers like Will Smith, Notorious B.I.G., LL Cool J, and Mariah Carey.

The Columbia contract was worth $250,000. 50 Cent received a $65,000 advance, but Jam Master took $50,000 of that initial payment. Some people claimed Jam Master got too much money for bringing a fresh new talent to Columbia Records, but 50 Cent has never felt that way. After becoming a star, he once said "[W]hat I learned from him is what allows me now to sell ten million records. He groomed me. That's worth $50,000."[21] Jam Master's share of the advance, however, left 50 Cent with very little cash. Although he was recording an album for Columbia, it would be nearly a year before it was released and he would start receiving royalties. Years later, an interviewer asked him what he did with the $15,000 he did get. Fifty replied that:

> I bought crack cocaine with it. Crack. Crack. I bought crack cocaine with it. How else you gonna provide for yourself? I did thirty-six songs in eighteen days for Columbia. Then I had eight months go by with no work going on.[22]

50 Cent had stopped selling drugs to follow his dream of becoming a rapper. But now he returned to drug dealing to make money until his album was released nearly a year later.

Rapper and Drug Dealer

When 50 Cent left the drug trade to pursue a rap career, he became so poor that he had to return to living with his grandparents. His son Marquise stayed with him there most of the time because Tompkins was busy attending college and working to support herself.

To fix his dire financial situation, 50 Cent began to sell drugs again. He purchased so much crack that he had to hire several people to help him sell and distribute the drug. In his autobiography, 50 Cent wrote: "When I got back into selling drugs, I was even more aggressive at it than I had been. I was picking up right where I had left off."[23] He hired several people to help him distribute and sell the drug and to protect his operation from other dealers in the area who resented his return to the drug scene.

During this period, 50 Cent also continued to make rap records to add to the ones he had already made for Columbia Records. After he signed with Columbia, company officials whisked 50 Cent away to a studio in upstate New York; in two-and-a-half weeks of nonstop work, he created thirty-six songs. Eighteen of the tunes were chosen for *Power Of The Dollar*, his debut album that was scheduled for release in 2000.

"How to Rob"

One of the songs 50 Cent made while waiting for his first album to come out was "How to Rob." When he released the record locally as a single in the summer of 1999, it began to make him famous. The song features a rapper who claims that if his records fail to make him successful, he will return to crime to support himself. The song's narrator then explains how he will steal from famous black rappers and singers like Will Smith, Puff Daddy, Whitney Houston, and Mariah Carey. 50 Cent saw the song as a way to make everyone know who he was right away, and it did. He also admitted that the thought of robbing rich people appealed to him at the time because he was poor. In an interview several years later, 50 Cent said:

> "I Rob" was the best thing I ever could think of. All I was doing with that record was makin' everybody at one time say "Who's 50 Cent? Who is this guy?" And it worked. Every interview that I speak on [since then] they mention that and ask me about it. [Well] when you're starvin', when robbery is not out of the question, it's easy to come up with that concept.[24]

He released another single called "Ghetto Qu'ran (Forgive Me)" which graphically described the work of drug dealers in Queens during the 1980s, a period of intense violence and growth in the drug trade. The song mentioned many of the criminals by name, including McGriff, Thomas "Tony Montana" Mickens, and

Eric "E Money Bags" Smith. Both records raised awareness of 50 Cent in the hip-hop community. But the songs also made a lot of people angry with him, including former drug dealers who did not like their bad deeds being brought to the public's attention. 50 Cent began to hear claims that some dealers wanted to kill him, but he ignored the rumors.

50 Cent is Almost Killed

At about 11 P.M. on the night of May 24, 2000, 50 Cent was sitting in the back seat of a friend's car parked in front of his grandmother's house. A second car pulled up alongside. A man got out, stepped to the vehicle, and began firing a nine-millimeter

50 Cent Gets Shot

5 0 Cent was shot nine times on May 24, 2000, while sitting in a car in front of his grandmother's home. In his autobiography, 50 Cent describes his near-fatal shooting:

I felt someone come over my shoulder [from outside the car] but saw no one there. [T]he shooter was sneaking up on my left side. I want to believe that I saw it coming at that point. But if I had seen it coming, then I wouldn't have got shot, would I? The shooter was on me, emptying bullets. I jumped. I felt my legs on fire and fell back down. The shooter stuck his hand deeper in the window, [his gun] still bucking. I reached for the jacket in my lap. I pointed the pistol at the shooter, but the gun wasn't cocked. There was nothing in the chamber. A bullet tore into my face and my mouth exploded. Another slug blew up my hand before the driver [and the gunman] finally pulled off.

50 Cent with Kris Ex, *From Pieces to Weight: Once Upon A Time in Southside Queens.* New York: MTV Books, 2005, p. 187.

pistol. 50 Cent was hit nine times, taking bullets in the hand, hip, and chest, with one bullet ripping through his left cheek and into his mouth. For 50 Cent, being shot was a strange experience: "You don't actually feel each one hit you. The adrenaline is pumping. You movin' and tryin' to get out of the way."[25] His friend drove him to Queens' Jamaica Hospital, where doctors stopped the bleeding from his multiple wounds and saved his life.

Road to Recovery

50 Cent was hospitalized for thirteen days and it took him months to recover. Although he escaped a life-threatening injury, it took a long time for 50 Cent to regain his strength. His weight had dropped from 230 pounds to 167 pounds, partly because his jaw was wired shut for nearly two months. At first he could only take food through an intravenous tube, and later could only eat macaroni and cheese and other soft food that had been run through a blender. Ever since his boxing days, 50 Cent had worked hard to keep in shape. He now had to retrain his body in the gym, especially his legs, since they had been struck several times by bullets.

50 Cent knew he had been lucky to live through the shooting, and he thought his survival was a sign that he was meant to do great things. He claims that "After I got shot nine times at close range and didn't die, I started to think that I must have a purpose in life, like, I have to be here for a reason."[26]

For awhile, however, 50 Cent was not sure if that destiny was to be a rap star. This was partly because of the way he was treated by his record company after his attempted murder.

Columbia Drops 50 Cent

50 Cent's dramatic brush with death helped secure his gangster image with rap fans. When they heard how 50 Cent survived the brutal attempt on his life, they believed he was a real-life tough guy. But executives at Columbia Records had a far different reaction to his shooting. As 50 Cent once explained it, "Columbia

got scared off when I got shot nine times. They didn't understand that I'd kept my day job [selling drugs]."[27]

The shooting made record company officials fear that 50 Cent was too controversial and could give their record label a bad image. Although no one knew for sure, the executives feared that 50 Cent had been shot because he had continued selling drugs. Officials were also worried that the money they spent promoting 50 Cent would be wasted if he was killed. After meeting with 50 Cent several times, Columbia executives told him they were not going to release *Power of the Dollar*.

Having his debut album canceled was harder on 50 Cent than being shot. In an interview, he once said:

> The most difficult thing I've experienced wasn't the shooting, it was being dropped by Columbia Records. It wasn't like I shot someone and they heard about it and they dropped me—they dropped me because I was shot. So, not only am I physically hurt, now I'm confused because I don't even know if I'm gonna be able to write music for a livin'.[28]

"No Use to Him Living"

Even though Columbia's rejection was a crippling blow to 50 Cent's dream of being a rapper, he continued to seek fame and fortune through singing. When 50 Cent made that decision, his grandmother realized that it was the right thing to do. Beulah Jackson, who had witnessed the shooting outside her home, said "I knew if he couldn't have his music, there was no use to him living."[29]

Chapter 3

50 Cent Becomes a Rap Superstar

ans of 50 Cent have little trouble recognizing their favorite rapper when they hear his records. 50 Cent has a very distinctive voice, one that is deep and smooth but with a slight slur when he says his words. This funny pronunciation is thanks to the nine-millimeter bullet that tore through his mouth when a gunman tried to kill him. The bullet's damaging route left the rapper with a square-shaped hole through the left side of his lower jaw. It destroyed a bottom tooth, and nicked a small chunk out of his gums. A minute bullet fragment is also still lodged in his tongue. These injuries make it harder for 50 Cent to say his words precisely. The rapper explains: "There's a different sound now when I talk [or sing], 'cause of the air around the tooth. Gettin' shot just totally fixed my instrument."[30]

But the murder attempt brought more than just a voice with a distinctive sound. It also made 50 Cent a legend to rap fans across the nation, and the popularity that grew out of that shocking incident helped him to become a star.

A Real Gangster Rapper

After 50 Cent survived the shooting, the news media and rap fans began comparing him to rap legend Tupac Shakur. Tupac became a star in 1991 with the release of his debut album *2Pacaplypse Now*. But when Tupac was shot five times during a brutal robbery attempt in New York City on November 30, 1994,

Tupac Shakur made gangster rap popular when he was alive and he continued to influence young rappers after he was murdered.

his status changed forever. By being tough enough to survive the shooting, Tupac became an icon; his popularity soared and he became more successful than ever.

Tupac invented the term "Thug Life" to describe the drug and crime scene in black inner city neighborhoods. He made gangster rap more popular than ever with songs that glorified drug use and criminals. Tupac was murdered in another shooting in Las Vegas on September 6, 1996, but he continued to influence young rappers long after his death. In the April 2005 edition of *Rolling Stone* magazine, 50 Cent wrote that "Every rapper who grew up in the nineties [1990s] owes something to Tupac."[31] And 50 Cent, more than most, owes a great deal to Tupac. He has borrowed the themes of inner city life that Tupac used in his songs as well as the rapper's flamboyant "thug" stage persona, complete with bulletproof vest and lots of diamond jewelry.

A Publishing Deal

50 Cent's biggest debt to the dead rapper, however, is that by surviving a brutal shooting as Tupac had done—he was even shot nine times, four more than Tupac—rap fans instantly rewarded him with a similar iconic status. The shooting also impressed a publishing firm, which believed the publicity surrounding the incident would help make 50 Cent a star when his debut album *Power of the Dollar* was released.

While 50 Cent was in the hospital recovering from his wounds, the publishing company signed him to write his autobiography. 50 Cent received a $125,000 advance for agreeing to do the book. The money helped him survive after Columbia Records canceled his contract and his debut album.

Becoming a Star Without a Contract

50 Cent was in career limbo after Columbia let him go. He had started to become famous because of the shooting and the popularity of his songs like "How to Rob". But his future as a rapper

50 Cent Had to Succeed

Many people were surprised 50 Cent was able to be a successful rapper after he was shot nine times. But in an interview with hip-hop journalist David "Davey D" Cook, 50 Cent said he had no other way to make something of himself other than a drug dealer:

> There was no Plan B for me. If I don't make music, I'm going back to the hood, I'll sell crack. I'm gonna go back to sell crack if I can't make it in the music business, and that's because that's what I was doing before that. I never had working papers, I never had a job. I sold crack until I got in the music, so this is the best thing that happened to me and I do it excessively. I make music 'cuz it's almost like I can escape everything I was involved in, alls I gotta do is make music. I put out four mixed tape albums waiting to release my real album [*Get Rich or Die Tryin'*]. I don't do nothin' but make music, you know what I mean?

Davey D Interview with 50 Cent January 8, 2003. Davey D's Hip Hop Corner. http://www.daveyd.com/interview50cent.html.

seemed in jeopardy because other record companies were afraid to sign someone who was dealing drugs and still at risk of being killed. Without the financial backing of a company to help him create and distribute albums, there seemed to be no way that he could become a successful rapper.

But 50 Cent refused to quit. He decided to try to make it in rap in an unconventional way. He made mix-tapes and inexpensive recordings of his own songs and added new lyrics to other people's songs. The mix-tapes were sold for a few dollars on street corners and in record shops. 50 Cent also gave some tapes to disc jockeys who played music at parties and to more than fifty radio stations across the country. He handed out the tapes for free in the hope that people would give him free exposure by playing them. This was a promotional trick 50 Cent had used as a drug dealer; he had sometimes given away crack samples to attract customers.

G-Unit

50 Cent knew he would not make much money on the mixtapes, but he realized it was the only way he could become a rap star without the backing of a major record label. He once explained the reasons behind his unusual plan for rap success:

In one of his songs, 50 Cent accused Kenneth "Supreme" McGriff, a drug dealer who started a record company, of being involved in his attempted murder.

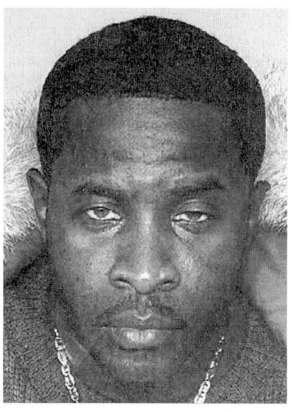

Mix-Tapes

50 Cent found an unusual way to become a successful rapper—mix-tapes. After Columbia Records canceled its contract with 50 Cent in 2000, no other company would sign him to a new one. The only way that 50 Cent could try to become popular as a rapper was to produce mix-tapes, CD collections of songs that individual artists can inexpensively record, produce, and distribute. 50 Cent started out by giving the mix-tapes to disc jockeys at radio stations so they would play them and make his songs known to many more people. He also sold the CDs on the street. 50 Cent was not the first would-be rapper who depended on mix-tapes to become a star. In the early 1990s, Notorious B.I.G. (Christopher Wallace) became successful by producing such tapes, and many young artists have done the same thing since then. Mix-tapes are cheaper to buy than albums produced by major record companies. Even though mix-tapes compete with the albums those companies sell, the record firms often provide material and help promote mix-tapes for singers they have signed. The companies do that to create more fans for their singers so that they will buy records in the future.

I started to work on music, putting it out on mix-tapes. The only business model I had was from selling drugs, so that's how I marketed my product. I knew that the only way to get into any market is to give out free samples. I had to build up a clientele before I could see a profit. I had to invest in my brand." [32]

The rap samples 50 Cent distributed came from a partnership he formed with Sha Money XL (Michael Clervoix III), an old friend. Sha Money had a recording studio in the basement of his home on Long Island, New York, and 50 Cent recorded mix-tapes there. He produced many mix-tapes, including four complete albums. He even featured other rappers on the tapes such as long-time friends Lloyd Banks and Tony Yayo. 50 Cent and the rappers he worked with became known as G-Unit, which was short for Guerrilla Unit. The name reflected the unconventional manner in which 50 Cent was trying to become a successful rapper.

50 Cent released his first mix-tape on May 21, 2002. It was called *Guess Who's Back?* and featured a song about his shooting. The song became famous in New York because it accused Kenneth "Supreme" McGriff of being involved in his attempted murder. In the song, 50 Cent wonders who shot him and he even lists possible suspects who might have played a part in the murder attempt, including McGriff. That song and others helped further establish 50 Cent's popularity among rap fans.

50 Cent's mix-tapes became so popular that they began outselling copies of major label records in inner city areas. That kind of success brought him into contact with two of the world's most famous and powerful rappers—Eminem (Marshall Bruce Mathers III) and Dr. Dre (Andre Romell Young).

Meeting Eminem and Dr. Dre

Eminem has sold more than 80 million albums worldwide and is the most popular white star in rap, music that is dominated by African Americans. Growing up in Detroit, Michigan, Mathers was drawn to music and began rapping as a teenager. Using the stage name Eminem, he achieved stardom in 1999 with the release of *The Slim Shady* album—Slim Shady is another of his nicknames. He has been a successful performer and producer ever since.

Eminem became interested in 50 Cent not only because he was a talented young rapper but because of his dramatic past. "His life story sold me," Eminem has said. "To have a story behind the music is so important."[33] Eminem understood how important that was because his own personal history helped him to achieve stardom. He was also wise enough to understand that 50 Cent's criminal past, including his surviving the shooting, gave 50 Cent credibility as a gangster rapper that few performers had ever had. Eminem said of 50 Cent that:

> When he talks about drugs and guns and death, you know he's speaking from experience. If he says he's gonna pop you

Eminem and Dr. Dre gave 50 Cent a record contract that started him on his way to fame and fortune.

[shoot you], you think he might. Kids wanna see a guy that got shot that many times and lived. There's a whole mystique about him." [34]

Shady/Aftermath

Eminem became a star after signing with Aftermath, a record label run by Dr. Dre (Andre Romell Young), a famous rapper and record producer. Dre used his experience to produce Eminem's first few albums. The two rap stars later formed Shady/Aftermath, a new company that produces records by many top rappers. They were so impressed with 50 Cent's mix-tapes that they wanted to sign him for their company. In June 2002, they flew him to Los Angeles so they could meet him.

The three rappers became friends, and 50 Cent started working with Dre to create rap songs. In just five days, 50 Cent and Dre produced seven new tunes, a tremendous burst of creativity. It did not take Dre long to realize how talented the young rapper was. "50, " he said, "is one of the most incredible artists I [have] worked with as far as writing, basic performance, and vibing."[35] 50 Cent was also impressed with Eminem and Dre. Best of all, they were willing to work with 50 Cent despite his past problems. He said that when they first met, "They asked was everything cool and I told them everything was cool. Then we just made music."[36]

The music led to big money as the famed rappers gave 50 Cent an advance of more than $1 million to sign a recording contract with them. Two years after Columbia Records had dropped him, 50 Cent was on his way to fame and fortune as a rapper.

50 Cent Gets Rich Without Dying

Eminem immediately put his new star to work. He had 50 Cent record "Wanksta," a song that 50 Cent had released on mix-tapes a year earlier, so it could be included on the soundtrack for the film *8 Mile*. The film, which was released in November 2002, was a fictional account of how Eminem became successful in the all-black world of rap.

"Wanksta" became 50 Cent's first commercial hit, climbing to No. 13 on *Billboard's* Hot 100 songs. In an interview in 2003 with hip-hop disc jockey Davey D. (David Cook), 50 Cent said how pleased he was that it was a success: "Wanksta, that's my joint right there, that's the first one [hit] that broke for me off the '8 Mile' [soundtrack]. I'm happy with that... it worked out for me, I'm blessed with that."[37]

Creating an Album

The song "Wanksta" was an attack on rapper Ja Rule, with whom 50 Cent has had a long-running feud. The song claims that unlike 50 Cent, Ja Rule and some other gangster rappers only pretend to be tough and have connections to crime and street life. Instead of "gangstas," 50 Cent claimed they were "wankstas."

50 Cent's first hit whetted his appetite for more success and he began working on *Get Rich or Die Tryin.'* The original release

50 Cent and rapper Ja Rule have had a long-running feud.

date for his debut album was February 11, 2003, but that was changed to February 6 to match the numerical police code for armed robbery (2-6). The album was a smash hit. Fans bought 872,000 copies the first week, 1.6 million in two weeks, and 6.5 million for the year. It was not only the year's best-selling album but the highest-selling debut album ever.

The album was widely praised. Even the sedate *New York Times* newspaper said the songs contained witty rhymes and dramatic story lines and that the album "seems to consist of nothing but hits."[38] One of those hits was "In Da Club," which became one of rap's greatest hits.

The Songs That Made 50 Cent A Star

"In Da Club" was released as a single before the album came out. On February 2, 2003, *Billboard*, the music industry's most influential magazine, reported that both "Wanksta" and "In Da Club" were in its top ten. That was the first time a singer had placed two songs so high in one week in three years.

Eminem and Dre co-produced the album. 50 Cent had come to them with thirty songs, which was enough for several albums. They helped him choose and refine the album's nineteen songs, including "What Up Gangsta," "P.I.M.P.," "Wanksta," and "Many Men," which claimed many men still wanted to kill 50 Cent. The album featured several other rappers, including Eminem, Young Buck, Lloyd Banks, and Tony Yayo.

Many of the songs capitalized on 50 Cent's dark reputation as a real-life gangster, which he knew was something that would help make him popular. But "In Da Club," the album's biggest hit, was a raucous party song that made people happy. It became *Billboard* magazine's top song of the year and helped the album become 2003's top album. Dre admitted later that he was amazed at how easy it was for 50 Cent to write the tune: "As soon as he walked in the studio, he picked up a pen, and we were done in an hour."[39]

50 Cent said "I just wanted to have some fun on this record," but he admitted the real enjoyment he got from it was its tremendous popularity: "When I see the response I'm getting from this record like when they go in [a] club and when they playin' it four or five times back to back, I'm like 'Yo ... that joint worked."[40]

50 Cent's Sense of Purpose

Sometimes when people survive serious injuries that could have killed them, they believe their lives have been spared because they are destined to do something important. 50 Cent felt that way after he was shot nine times and lived. He explains that it helped him believe he could do something positive with his life:

> I think I [survived because] I'm supposed to do something positive, more positive. The fact that I exist is saying there's always a possibility [of doing greater things]. There's always hope... I got shot nine times. The big deal is you start thinking that he shot you nine times and didn't finish you—that makes you feel like you have a purpose, a reason for being. Besides the fool being a shooter [a professional killer], you gotta feel God made the shells land where they land, so I look at all my situations and everything I go through [and] I'm still trying to figure out what my purpose is; I think it's something positive.

Jake Brown, *50 Cent: No Holds Barred.* Phoenix. AZ: Colossus Books, 2005, p. 54.

It Was 50 Cent's Time

It took 50 Cent a long time to have that kind of success. But when it came, 50 Cent was philosophical about the hardships he had to endure to make it as a rapper: "See, if I wasn't blessed with the opportunity to come with the timing that I came, the world might not have been ready for 50 Cent."[41]

Chapter 4

The Ultimate Gangster Rapper

It took 50 Cent years to learn to rap and to have his first album produced and distributed by a major record company like Shady/Aftermath. But when *Get Rich or Die Tryin'* was released on February 6, 2003, the young rapper immediately skyrocketed to fame and fortune. Rap fans flooded record stores to buy his debut album, which sold 872,000 copies the first week and 12 million by the end of the year. Hit singles from the album like "Wanksta" and "In Da Club" became some of the most oft-played songs on radio stations across the country.

World Tours

50 Cent's amazing success transformed him overnight into one of rap's biggest stars. He began touring around the nation and the world, and his concerts were sell-outs. Radio stations interviewed him and newspapers and magazines ran countless stories about how a former drug dealer who had survived a murder attempt was now a singing sensation. His picture, usually a head shot of 50 Cent glaring at readers with a menacing expression, appeared on the covers of magazines and in newspapers across the country. In May 2003, the nationally distributed newspaper *USA Today* ran a long story about his life. Reporter Steve Jones began the article this way:

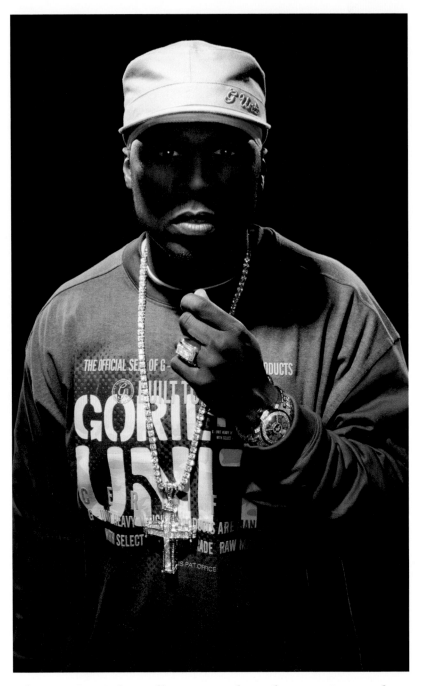

After 50 Cent's first album was released, magazines and newpapers across the country ran stories of his life.

In three short months, rapper 50 Cent has gone from "who?" to "wow!", selling 4 million albums and appearing on three of the ten most-heard songs on the radio this week. He may be new to the mainstream, but he is only the latest—and surely not the last—in a long line of rappers who have gangstered their way to mass appeal."[42]

The *USA Today* article noted that 50 Cent had become successful by following in the footsteps of "gangsta" rappers like

The Appeal of Gangster Rap

The amazing success 50 Cent had with *Get Rich or Die Tryin'* gave new life to gangster rap. In an article in *USA Today*, reporter Steve Jones quoted several people who tried to explain why rappers are so popular:

Manny Fresh of the Big Tymers, [a singer] who made "bling-bling" part of the everyday language, says thugs move through life with an air of confidence most people would like to emulate. "Bad boys always win in everything," says Fresh. "It's like a Hollywood story. The girl always wants to be with the bad boy because your parents always tell you not to." Motown [record company] president Kedar Massenberg says [gangster rap] music sells because it feeds into the nation's long-standing fixation [interest] with shady characters in general. "There just happens to be a lot more people who are caught up in the thug image than are caught up in a Will Smith [wholesome] image," Massenberg says. "America was built on scandals, and when you try to be too squeaky-clean, it never sells."

Steve Jones, "Carrying on the gangsta mystique, trends come and go, but thug life endures." *USA Today*, May 23, 2003, E1.

Tupac Shakur, Ice-T (Tracy Marrow), the Notorious B.I.G. (Christopher Wallace), Jay-Z (Shawn Corey Carter), and Ja Rule (Jeffrey Atkins). "Gangsta" rappers are those who used their songs to glorify what Shakur called "thug life," the gritty inner city lifestyle that includes drug use, crime, violence, and easy sex. A major factor in 50 Cent's rise to stardom in "gangsta" rap was that he had actually been a criminal; he had sold drugs, engaged in gun fights, been convicted of drug charges, and served sentences in correctional facilities.

50 Cent realized how important his dark past was to his success. And despite his impressive gangster resumé, he used the news media to enhance that image.

50 Cent Polishes His Gangster Image

The stories journalists wrote about 50 Cent after his album came out focused on his criminal past because it was so unusual for a drug dealer to become a hit singer. The drug world is violent, and reporters often asked 50 Cent if he had ever killed anyone. 50 Cent denied being a murderer, but acknowledged that he would not own up to such a crime if he had committed murder because he would leave himself open to investigation by the police. 50 Cent liked to add some mystery when he answered these questions because it often led people to believe that he might have killed someone.

When interviewers asked about being shot in 2002, which they always did, 50 Cent again used the dramatic event to add to his tough guy image. For example, 50 Cent always mentioned that the person who shot him was dead. He told one reporter, "He got killed. Freak accident. He got killed a few weeks after I got shot. Same situation, somebody waiting on him."[43] The way 50 Cent laughed when he answered the question made it seem as if he might have been involved in killing his attacker. Police believe the man who shot 50 Cent was Darryl Braun, a violent criminal whose nickname was "Hommo," short for "homicide." Braun was gunned down nearly three weeks after the shooting, but police say his killing was not related to the attempt on 50 Cent's life.

50 Cent the Bad Guy

However, 50 Cent kept bringing up Braun's death in an attempt to link himself to such violence. He did that because he understood that his dark image helped make him popular. 50 Cent once explained his theory about why his fans liked people like him:

> I think kids like me like the bad guy in a film. People love the bad guy. I watch movies all the time and root for the bad guy and turn it off before it ends because the bad guy dies. It's cinematic law: The bad guy has to die. But sometimes the bad guy gets a record deal and becomes a superstar like 50.[44]

Songs in his debut album such as "In Da Club," "P.I.M.P.," "Wanksta," and "Many Men (Wish Death)" reinforced the bad guy image 50 Cent had lived and was now trying to enhance for his new fans. Although the *New York Times* newspaper said his album "seems to consist of nothing but hits," the review also noted that the lyrics in the songs were dark: "It's a grim party: The casual jokes about death are his way of reminding us of the price he might have to pay for his success—and for our entertainment."[45]

50 Cent's Debut Album

Get Rich or Die Tryin' created a revival of "gangsta rap." In a review for the *Star Tribune* in Minneapolis, Minnesota, Chris Riemenschneider wrote: "Not since the 1996–97 murders of rappers Tupac Shakur and the Notorious B.I.G. [Christopher Wallace] has mainstream hip-hop been so filled with guns, gang-style feuds and songs about killing."[46] After both singers were gunned down in separate incidents, the lyrics in "gangsgta rap" songs had grown

Rapper the Notorious B.I.G. was gunned down within several months of Tupac Shakur's murder.

a bit tamer and less violent as a reaction to the sensational shootings that stunned everyone in the rap world.

50 Cent felt that he was justified in reusing violent imagery in his songs because he had been involved in real-life episodes of the violence he sang about, most famously the failed attempt to kill him. The fact that 50 Cent survived the shooting helped to make him a heroic figure. That was something he never wanted his fans to forget, and he keeps mentioning the key incident in his life in his songs. In "Many Men (Wish Death)," 50 Cent boasts that he is still alive even though people had wanted him dead. And even "In Da Club," which is basically a party song, he refers to the limp he still has from the shooting. He further polishes his tough guy image in "What Up Gangsta?," when the song's narrator boasts of having $100,000 stashed away as well as a machine gun to protect the money he made illegally.

Initial Reviews

The album's success, however, was not only due to his status as a gangster and the sensational lyrics. In a review in *Time* magazine, Josh Tryangiel complimented 50 Cent's singing by writing "he happens to be very good, particularly at setting a mood with his rumbling baritone."[47] 50 Cent's voice was deep and smooth, even when delivering lyrics about killing people. But Eminem (Marshall Bruce Mathers III) believes the real secret to 50 Cent's success is that no matter what words he sang, people believed him:

> One of the things that excited me about Tupac, was even if he was rhymin' the simplest words in the world, you felt like he meant it and it came from his heart. That's the thing with 50. That same aura. That's been missing since we lost Pac and Biggie. The authenticity, the realness behind it.[48]

Not all the reviews were positive. *Chicago Sun-Times* critic Jim DeRogatis claimed 50 Cent did not have "a tenth of Tupac's talent" and dismissed him as "a lazy, thick-tongued rapper whose themes are tiresome and whose rhyming skills are poor at best."[49]

A Review of *The Massacre*

50 Cent's first two albums were generally well received. In a review of *The Massacre*, the influential music magazine *Rolling Stone* praised both 50 Cent's personality and his singing voice:

> It helps that 50 Cent is the most likable rapper ever to need a bulletproof vest. Like his Kevlar-wearing predecessor and idol, Tupac Shakur, 50 Cent has charisma up the muzzle-hole. But where Tupac could be manic and unpredictable, 50 Cent is cool and easy to be around— you get the sense that if he weren't so busy getting shot, stabbed, and selling millions of albums, he would be an enormously successful fraternity president or restaurateur.... As always, 50 Cent's secret weapon is his singing voice—the deceptively amateur-sounding tenor croon that he deploys on almost every chorus here. 50 Cent knows perfectly the limitations of his voice—he stays within his register and more than makes up in personality what he lacks in technique. Unlike many rappers who sing off-key with perverse joy, 50 Cent shows a jazzy touch when he sings the title hook to "God Gave Me Style."

Nathan Brackett, "50 Cent: The Massacre." *Rolling Stone*, March 10, 2005, p. 107.

Reviews like that, however, failed to stop fans from making 50 Cent a superstar by buying millions of copies of his album.

50 Cent would not release his next album—*The Massacre*— for nearly two years because he was busy performing concerts, acting, and getting involved in other business ventures. To promote *The Massacre*, 50 Cent and other G-Unit rappers broadcast live on WQHT, a New York hip-hop radio station known as the "Hot 97" for a whole weekend. In one segment, 50 Cent kept repeating one line from a song over and over while scratching a

record and comparing himself to two famous Queens criminals. The references let his fans know that his new album would have the same themes about "thug life" as his first.

Another Huge Hit

The album cover for *The Massacre* had the muscular 50 Cent posing like a Mutant Ninja Turtle—he and his son, Marquise, are both fans of the cartoon characters. Thanks to hit songs like "Candy Shop," "Outta Control," and "I'm Supposed To Die Tonight," it sold 1.4 million copies in just four days and became the bestselling album in the United States, United Kingdom, Australia, and even Sweden. The album included performances by G-Unit rappers Tony Yayo, Lloyd Banks, Young Buck, and Olivia.

Heroin As a Lover

The *Massacre*, 50 Cent's second album, includes a song called "A Baltimore Love Thing," which is about heroin addiction. 50 Cent was very proud of the song. In this excerpt from a biography about him, the rapper explains what the song is about:

> One of my favorite songs is "A Baltimore Love Thing." It's titled that because in Baltimore the heroin addiction rate is really high. So the song is about the relationship between an addict and the drug. I give this drug emotion, feelings and at some point in the song, the drug actually becomes mad at the addict for trying to leave. It's like a real vivid description of what it would be like if it was human. You hear people make references to drugs talking and people who are addicted to it.

Jake Brown, *50 Cent: No Holds Barred*. Phoenix. AZ: Colossus Books, 2005, p. 171.

50 Cent used many songs to reinforce his tough-guy image. In "I'm Supposed to Die Tonight," he dramatically details the night he was shot and talks about how blood flowed from his many wounds. On "This Is 50," he sings about how he hates rappers who are trying to imitate him and claims he has enough ammunition to kill every one of them.

The album, however, is not all about violence and death. "Candy Shop," which 50 Cent sings with Olivia, is a high-spirited party tune whose many references to eating various kinds of candy are thinly-veiled references to sex. In "Baltimore Love Thing," 50 Cent comments seriously about drug addiction. 50 Cent describes heroin addiction as a relationship between two people that involves both love and hate, which is a realistic definition of addiction. 50 Cent said the creative way that he wrote about addiction showed how he had changed since his debut album:

> I wanted songs that represented growth from the last album to this one. On *Get Rich or Die Tryin*,' I would have written that song like I was selling heroin. But on *The Massacre*, I'm dealing with deeper issues. The way I choose to express myself is new. I picked up the pieces I missed on the first album.[50]

50 Cent had not, however, outgrown his need to mock other rappers. In "Piggy Bank," he continued his almost constant flow of verbal assaults against Ja Rule and other rappers.

Rapping Other Rappers

Rap music is known for its "beefs," the long-term feuds rappers have to mock their competitors. The beefs are conducted through lyrics in records, verbal taunts during concerts, and music videos. The most famous beef was the long-running war in the 1990s between East Coast and West Coast rappers. Tupac, who was from California, was at the center of the feud between the two sets of rappers. Notorious B.I.G. was also involved, and there is speculation that the murders of both rappers were due to the ill feeling the rap war generated. Ja has always been one of 50 Cent's favorite targets. They were both from Queens, which made them naturally jealous of each other's success. In addition, 50 Cent always believed that Ja was only pretending to be a gangsta rapper. Ja was raised in middle-class comfort, not hard-core poverty, and at five feet three inches (1.6m) the slight singer did not seem to fit gangsta rap's tough image. 50 Cent has humorously compared Ja to Sesame Street's Cookie Monster and on "Wanksta" he ridiculed Ja for claiming to be a "gangsta" but having never committed any crimes or violence like a real gangster. The record mentioned other rappers that 50 Cent felt were wankstas, which was his term for people pretending to be gangsters.

50 Cent has had beefs with dozens of rappers, including the Game (Jayceon Taylor), Cam'ron (Cameron Giles), Nas (Nasir Jones), Diddy (Sean John Combs), and Li'l Kim (Kimberly Denise Jones). 50 Cent believes that beefs are a good way to weaken or eliminate his competition, something he always tried to do as a drug dealer. "We hustle until we get enough finances and manpower and start moving ... [dealers] off the strip," is the way 50 Cent once explained how he took territory from rival drug dealers.[51] Beefs were his tactic to do the same thing to other rappers.

However, many rap beefs (including some involving 50 Cent) seem to be designed to create media publicity so the feuding singers can sell more records. The beef between 50 Cent and Game, for example, peaked just before *The Massacre* was released; they declared a truce in their war on March 9, 2005, but not before the bitter exchanges helped publicize 50 Cent's new album.

50 Cent's "Sappy Love Song"

The beefs helped 50 Cent strengthen his tough guy image. However, the rapper sometimes displayed a more mellow side in his songs. The tune "21 Questions" on *Get Rich or Die Tryin'* is a sentimental love song. 50 Cent admitted that Dr. Dre (Andre Romell Young), who coordinated the album, did not want the song on his debut effort because it interfered with the gangster image Shady/Aftermath was trying to create for him. 50 Cent said:

> Dre was, like, "How you goin' to be gangsta this and that and then put this sappy love song on?" But I told him, "I'm two people. I've always had to be two people since I was a kid, to get by. To me that's not diversity, it's necessity." [52]

50 Cent's insistence on including the song showed that even the ultimate gangster rapper was not entirely a tough guy.

Chapter 5

50 Cent the Rapper Businessman

When Curtis began selling crack cocaine as a twelve-year-old boy, he was motivated by more than just a desire to have the expensive clothes and athletic shoes his grandparents could not buy him. Curtis was also led into drug dealing by a character trait that has dominated his life—his restless desire to constantly test himself in new ventures. As a teenager, Curtis tried to become a boxer even though he was busy selling drugs and going to school. This is how 50 Cent once explained that part of his personality:

> I've always been ambitious. I don't think ambition is a learned behavior. I think it's a part of a person's character. Some people just have that drive. Even if I've accomplished a million things, I'll be trying to accomplish a million and one. My goals change as I move forward. I get excited about the next thing."[53]

That driving ambition pushed 50 Cent into other business ventures even after he began making millions of dollars as a rapper. 50 Cent began acting in movies, performing concerts, running his own record label and clothing company, and publishing fiction books about inner city life. He helped create the video game *50 Cent: Bulletproof* and began marketing flavored water. But of all the businesses that grew out of his singing, making movies got him the most attention.

50 Cent the Movie Star

50 Cent's first film *Get Rich or Die Tryin'* was released on November 9, 2005. Like the 2002 movie *8 Mile*, which fictionalized the life of rapper Eminem (Marshall Bruce Mathers III), the film combined elements of 50 Cent's life with made-up events to create a dramatic story. Many details of the film's plot came from 50 Cent's autobiography—*From Pieces to Weight: Once Upon A Time in Southside Queens*—which was published August 9, 2005.

Get Rich or Die Tryin' was a fictionalized version of 50 Cent's life.

50 Cent's Movie Biography

The film *Get Rich or Die Tryin'* is based on 50 Cent's life. Even though the film was about what happened to him, it was not always easy for 50 Cent to act in the movie:

> Some people think because you're making a film that's based on your life story that you're not actually acting, ya know, but I still gotta deliver the dialogue like everybody else. One of [the hardest] was the actual operating scene. I spent eight hours that day and something like a minute of it was in the film. I had prosthetics and make-up on me, so I couldn't move, and I'm looking up at the lights that you could see in the operating room, I got actors over me delivering dialogue, doing a great job at acting like surgeons, and when they say cut, everyone's laughing and doing what they doing, but like I can't move off the table! And it's like, I been in that position before, just I wasn't conscious, I was under anesthesia at that point. So now I have a reference in my head to what would have happened after I was shot and unconscious.

Lauren Saft, "An Interview with 50 Cent." Club Planet Archives, November 4, 2005. www.clubplanet.com/news/archive/the_50_cent_interview.asp.

The book and movie script were written at the same time; 50 Cent and Kris Ex, who co-authored the memoir, worked with screenwriter Terry Winter.

The character 50 Cent played was Marcus, a young man who—like 50 Cent just a few years earlier—was trying to quit selling drugs and become a rapper. In the movie's opening scene, Marcus is nearly killed in a shooting incident that mimics the most famous incident in 50 Cent's life. 50 Cent claims that even though some events in the movie never happened to him, about three-quarters of the film is true to his life story:

> It was difficult to create a film that captures all of that energy accurately in one little, you know, hour and a half. How do you put your life—I'm 29 years old—into an hour and a half? [But] everything that's there is relevant to my life, it's just, it's gumbo [a combination]."[54]

Acting the Part

Acting came naturally to 50 Cent because he grew up pretending to be two people—a hardened criminal on the streets and a loving grandson at home. But 50 Cent discovered acting could be difficult even though he was playing a character based on himself. The hardest thing for 50 Cent was to show emotion by crying, something he had never allowed himself to do because it would have made his enemies think he was weak. 50 Cent explained that "I had anxiety about having to get that done [in the film]. What helped me cry in that scene was me thinking about people viewing me as a failure."[55] The mental trick worked because failing to succeed at anything was his worst nightmare.

50 Cent's debut performance won the praise of movie critic Roger Ebert, who wrote that "Jackson is a good actor, at least in this film, playing himself."[56] His starring role also earned him a part in *Home of the Brave*, a movie about the Iraq War. It was released December 15, 2006, and also starred Samuel L. Jackson and Jessica Biel. 50 Cent played Jamal Aiken, a soldier who has trouble adapting to life after returning from fighting in Iraq. Playing a combat soldier who could be killed any day reminded 50 Cent of the danger he had experienced daily as a drug dealer. That knowledge helped him understand how the fear of dying could change a soldier:

> So, can you imagine waking up in the morning and somebody's not in the bunk next to you? Your imagination says, "One of these days." You have to take into account that it's happening all around you, that one day your bunk is going

*50 Cent's first movie led to a part in **Home of the Brave** with Samuel L. Jackson.*

to be empty; that you will be the person that don't make it back. I believe that would change a person's spirit."[57]

Although 50 Cent enjoyed acting, his first love was rapping. Only now, 50 Cent was running his own record label instead of just singing himself.

50 Cent and G-Unit

50 Cent was able to combine acting and rapping while filming *Get Rich or Die Tryin'*. When 50 Cent was not shooting scenes for the movie, he was writing lyrics for songs on its soundtrack. The soundtrack had the same title as his first album, but 50 Cent was quick to point out that it was nothing like his debut piece:

> I based the original *Get Rich or Die Tryin'* on my life and my moods at that point [but for the soundtrack] I used the actual scenes to create the things in the record. There's a scene where young Marcus is looking through a storefront window at sneakers, and at that point he was "window shoppin'" and that's what created the concept for the single off the soundtrack. I wrote it from 50 Cent's perspective as opposed to the character's."[58]

The G-Unit is made up of friends who are also rappers.

"Window Shopper" is about rappers looking at jewelry and cars they cannot afford, a universal theme everyone can understand. In the song, 50 Cent pokes fun at fellow rappers like Ja Rule (Jeffrey Atkins) by naming them as the window shoppers. As with his first two albums, rappers Tony Yayo and Lloyd Banks were guest artists with their own songs. They are only two members of G-Unit, the group of rappers 50 Cent works with regularly. As a group, G-Unit has been so successful that Interscope, the parent company of Shady/Aftermath, gave 50 Cent his own G-Unit record label.

Loyalty to old friends is a major reason that 50 Cent formed G-Unit. He knew Yayo and Banks before he became famous, and Banks said they knew 50 Cent would help them be successful when he became a star: "We knew that the moment he made it that we'd made it because he was always the older brother."[59] The partnership thrives, however, on more than friendship. Yayo said the three friends and other G-Unit members stimulate each other creatively to do their best work. He said it works this way: "We're competitive, 'cause that keeps you on your toes. Banks has [the] hottest punch lines in New York. He'll say a hot punch line and [then] 50 Cent comes with some fire and then I know I gotta write some [good material]."[60]

The songs 50 Cent and his G-Unit rap colleagues create are heard not only on CD players and radio stations. They are also sung at live concerts all over the world.

50 Cent Tours the World

In addition to his many appearances in the United States, 50 Cent has rapped in Europe, Asia, and Africa. One of 50 Cent's most memorable trips abroad came in the fall of 2005 when he visited Iraq to perform for U.S. soldiers. He went there from South Africa, where he was doing a series of concerts. Many of the young soldiers in Iraq enjoy hip-hop music and were grateful the rappers came to entertain them. The trip to Iraq, however, was dangerous. 50 Cent explains what happened to him:

> When I was performing for the troops in war-torn Iraq, the first thing one of the American soldiers said to me was: "I'm not going to [lie to] you, but you could die today." Just then, as he finished speaking, the bombs started going off. We couldn't leave so they had to re-schedule my flight out of the war zone. I was trapped there for five hours. And, after what the soldier had said to me, I was so grateful just to be able to leave on a plane as soon as possible.[61]

Even though rap was created in the United States by black inner city youths, it has become popular around the world. 50 Cent admits he enjoys taking the American art form to other countries. When 50 Cent played in Bangkok, Thailand, in March 2006, he said "I'm more excited about performing here than

Because rap has become popular around the world,
50 Cent enjoys performing in other countries.

I would be in New York [because] it's so common to them. They're excited about it [New Yorkers], but it's not as ground-breaking to them [as for Thai people]."[62] When he gave a concert for 10,000 people in Jerusalem, Israel, in June 2006, 50 Cent finished the concert by saying "Shalom [peace], everybody."[63] Israeli hip-hop artists Keleh 6 and Subliminal opened the concert, which showed how popular rap is in Israel.

Language Barrier

Many of the people attending 50 Cent's concerts in foreign countries do not speak English, and those who do speak the language often have trouble understanding slang words and cultural references in his songs. However, fans still enjoy listening to 50 Cent even if they have trouble translating his songs. When 50 Cent performed in Kiev, Ukraine, in June 2006, Olha Ponomarchuk said she found his music sexy and liked his voice. Ponomarchuk said "He sings about drugs, sex, criminality. I don't really listen to his music for the words, but more for his rhythms."[64] One reason Ukrainians like rap is because themes in the songs are similar to those in "shanson." This is a Russian style of music whose lyrics describe people who live in poverty, endure many tragedies, and often become involved in crime.

50 Cent has also performed throughout the United States. His concerts are dramatic, with unique stage sets like one that showed New York City in ruins, including the Statue of Liberty with her head cut off. The rapper likes to make his concerts interesting. In January 2005, a false report claimed that his left hand had been cut off when a door on his Cadillac Escalade closed on it. At a performance in New York soon after that, 50 Cent walked onto the stage with his hand encased in bandages and his arm in a sling. The crowd was stunned until he tore off the sham wrappings. 50 Cent enjoyed the joke he had played: "You should have seen [the audience's] faces. I never had so much fun in my life."[65]

50 Cent has performed in unusual places to attract new fans. After an auto race in June 2004 at Rockingham speedway in Corby, England, 50 Cent entertained more than 20,000 people.

50 Cent's concerts are dramatic and interesting.

Mike Lighty, who helps arrange promotional events for 50 Cent, said "This was a different market for him. You don't see too many rappers at stock car races."[66] Lighty said 50 Cent would like to do similar events at U.S. auto races to help broaden his fan base.

The rapper was paid well for performing at the race. Equally as important for 50 Cent, however, was the opportunity to make new fans who would buy his records, go to his movies, and enrich him through his other business ventures.

The Business Man

When 50 Cent became famous as a rapper, he used his celebrity to make money in ways other than selling records. Jimmy Iovine is president of Interscope Records, the company that gave 50 Cent his own record label. He claims that 50 Cent is "one of the best businessmen I've ever worked with. He's got a game plan for whatever happens."[67] 50 Cent used that business sense to appeal to his fan base by starting a clothing line and a series of novels about inner city life. He also allowed his name to be used to sell athletic shoes, jewelry, watches, and even flavored water.

50 Cent started G-Unit Books to publish gritty novels about inner city life.

50 Cent the Businessman

50 Cent's success as a rapper has allowed him to make money in many ways. But whether 50 Cent is acting in movies, selling G-Unit logo clothing, or advertising vitamin water, his business interests are all motivated by the same urge that once drove him to sell drugs—making money. To help him achieve that goal 50 Cent hired Chris Lighty, who has managed the business interests of other rappers. Lighty, a former rapper himself, arranges business deals for 50 Cent. In a newspaper interview in 2007, Lighty said rappers need to find new sources of income because future sales of their records are endangered by new technology that allows consumers to get music for free. Said Lighty: "As music sales go down because kids are stealing it off the Internet and trading it [to each other] and iPod sales continue to rise, you can't rely on just the income that you would make off of [records]."

Chris Lighty, a former rapper, manages 50 Cent's business interests.

50 Cent: Bulletproof is a video game based, in part, on 50 Cent's life story.

Nekesa Mumbi Moody, "Rap's deal guru makes sure it's not all about music." *Milwaukee Journal-Sentinel*, April 19, 2007, p. B6.

In January 2007, 50 Cent launched G-Unit Books in a joint venture with MTV/Pocket Books. He is listed as co-author on novels with titles such as *Death Before Dishonor, Baby Brother*, and *The Ski Mask Way*. The novels are harsh tales about inner city life that include graphic violence and sex. 50 Cent believes the books put in print the kind of stories he usually sings about. He said:

> Now I'm rounding up some of the top writers, same way I rounded up some of the top rappers in the game. The stories in the G-Unit series are the kinds of dramas me and my crew have been dealing with our whole lives; it's about our life on the streets, and no one knows it better than us."[68]

Marketing Products

50 Cent realized hip-hop fans want to dress like their favorite rappers. In 2003, he teamed with Mark Ecko, the founder of Ecko Unlimited, to create the G-Unit Clothing Company. Clothes and Reebok shoes marketed under his name are made for adults and children. The watches that bear his name run from inexpensive timepieces to the G-Unit MP3, which costs several hundred dollars because it can download and play up to sixteen hours of music (in the 256 MB model). The high-tech watch includes earbud headphones and can connect to computers via a USB port to download songs.

The rapper also capitalized financially on his fans' love for video games. He helped create *50 Cent: Bulletproof*, which can be played on Sony PlayStation and Microsoft Xbox. In *Bulletproof*, 50 Cent and members of his G-Unit record label like Banks and Yayo battle New York criminals. There are even brief appearances by Eminem and Dr. Dre. The game is very violent, but 50 Cent defends it by saying:

> The game is aggressive, so I can see how some may interpret it as glorifying the gangster lifestyle, but many parts of it are based on my life story. Many people know I was shot nine times [in 2000], so that's just the way it is.[69]

50 Cent's Video Game

In 2005, 50 Cent starred in the video game *50 Cent: Bulletproof*. 50 Cent did not just want to lend his name to the game—he wanted to be a part of creating it to make sure his fans would like it. He explains how he narrated the game and was filmed for hours to allow animators to create life-like images of him:

[I] spent twenty hours doing voice-over. I had to do the motion, when you put on the suit, the motion suit. I did all kinds of work with them on the actual video game.... You know what, I spend so much time on the tour bus—I watch [my friends] spend maybe four or five hours [playing video games] while we're going from city to city. So I just wanted to be a part of that form of entertainment. And that's why I'm actually in the video game as opposed to just making the videogame and saying 50 Cent or G-Unit videogames, just putting all my music in it. [And] then there are four new records that I wrote for the actual video game.

Jeff Otto, Interview: "50 Cent." September 6, 2005. IGN (Imagine Games Network) www.movies.ign.com/articles/647/647683p1.html.

To people who do not know 50 Cent, it might seem strange for a rap star to endorse flavored water because many rappers have a reputation for drinking alcohol, not water. But 50 Cent, who does not drink, rejected several offers to promote alcoholic beverages. He chose Glaceau Vitamin Water because he drinks it himself. He even helped the company create Formula 50, a grape-flavored water named after him that has 50 percent of the recommended daily allowance of vitamins. The rapper has been featured in advertisements showing him drinking Glaceau at home.

50 Cent believes so strongly in Glaceau that he bought stock in the company. When he purchased part of the firm in 2005, 50 Cent had plenty of money to make such an investment.

50 Cent endorses, and drinks, a flavored vitamin water instead of alcohol.

Making Money Legally

Although 50 Cent grew up in poverty, believing that selling drugs was the only way he could make any money, he has now become a multimillionaire through sales of CD albums, concerts, and his many business deals. But even though 50 Cent has made enough money to be set for life, he continues to try to make his fortune grow even larger. He says: "Selling a CD or a pair of sneakers won't get you arrested. Which means my work ethic should be even harder." [70]

Chapter 6

A 50 Cent Lifestyle

50 Cent released his third album on June 26, 2007. It was titled *Curtis*, the real first name of the rapper who was born Curtis James Jackson III. Many people were surprised that 50 Cent used his legal name instead of the stage name he has made famous. However, 50 Cent explained there was an important reason to do that:

> You ever seen *Batman Begins*? This album is like that for me as an artist. [The] record falls somewhere between *Get Rich or Die Tryin'* and *The Massacre* because of [its] content. That's why I titled the album *Curtis*, because it was prior to the world knowing me as 50 Cent.[71]

The Batman movie details how Bruce Wayne became a superhero who fights crime. 50 Cent claims that his new album explains his origins from his drug-dealing days when he was known as Curtis. For example, the song "Fully Loaded Clip" includes lines that refer to how he used to prepare drugs for sale and kept his nine-millimeter pistol shined up so it looked good. Although these lyrics are reminders of his past, the title of another song, "Straight to the Bank," better describes 50 Cent's current lifestyle because he has made so much money since his days as a hustler.

A Millionaire's Lifestyle

50 Cent grew up in poverty, crowded into a small home with his grandparents and eight uncles and aunts. Today he owns homes in several cities and lives like the multimillionaire he has become,

50 Cent tries to be a good dad and provides Marquise and his mother a house in Long Island.

thanks to his album sales, movie roles, concerts, and business ventures. In 2003, he purchased the home of former heavyweight boxing champion Mike Tyson in Farmington, Connecticut, for $4.1 million. The mansion had fifty-two rooms, including eighteen bedrooms, twenty-five bathrooms, and an elevator. The rapper spent $6 million to remodel the house, which included adding a helicopter landing pad.

The rapper also owns houses in Long Island, New York, and Baltimore, Maryland. The Long Island house is where Shaniqua Tompkins lives with their son, Marquise. 50 Cent never knew his father and is trying to be a good dad; he reportedly bought the home because Long Island has a good school system. Marquise, who has been nicknamed "25 Cent," often travels with 50 Cent and has appeared on stage with him in concerts. 50 Cent was once asked if he was a strict father. The rapper jokingly said, "Nah, he's spoiled. I don't think there's enough spoiled black kids, you know what I mean?"[72]

Relationships

50 Cent and Shaniqua never married; 50 Cent supports her financially but they live apart. This allows 50 Cent to date other women, including celebrities such as actress Vivica Fox, with whom he attended the 2003 MTV Awards. When 50 Cent dated Fox, he discovered that being famous has one big drawback—attention from the news media. He said "We'd go out and all of a sudden there would be photographers there, like on cue."[73] 50 Cent was pursued by journalists and photographers wherever he went. He eventually broke up with Fox because he thought she was dating him to get publicity to boost her career.

50 Cent's new wealth enables him to go to exclusive nightclubs and high profile sports events. As a former boxer, he enjoys attending heavyweight title bouts and has become friends with Tyson and other fighters. When 50 Cent travels to other cities, for business or for pleasure, he goes by private plane. If 50 Cent wants to drive somewhere, he can choose one of many luxury

Actress Vivica Fox is one of a number of celebrities 50 Cent has been seen with.

vehicles he owns, such as a Cadillac Escalade or a Lamborghini, a foreign sports car that costs $300,000.

Several armed guards accompany 50 Cent wherever he goes. In 2003, photographer Albert Watson took 50 Cent's picture for the cover of *Rolling Stone* magazine. 50 Cent seemed so nice that Watson was surprised the rapper needed protection; he also had trouble believing someone had once tried to kill him. Watson told him, "You're the nicest guy in the world. Who would want to put all these bullets in you?" Watson remembered how 50 Cent replied: "He looked at me with a smile and said, 'Well, I wasn't always a nice guy.'"[74]

Danger and Violence Surround 50 Cent

The rapper needs bodyguards because he has enemies who want to harm him. He wears a bulletproof vest for the same reason. "Yeah, I put it on right after my underwear," he once said in an interview.[75] 50 Cent believes he developed dangerous enemies through his days as a criminal and the "beefs" he has conducted against other rappers. "My past is my shadow. Wherever I go, it's going to go with me," is the way 50 Cent explains past actions that continue to place him in danger.[76]

His past came back to haunt him when Jam Master Jay (Jason Mizell) was shot to death November 2, 2002, while sitting in a van in the Bronx, New York. Police questioned 50 Cent about the murder because they believed his former mentor might have been killed because of his association with the rap star. 50 Cent said police also told him about reports they have received that people still want to kill him. He himself admitted that:

> I know that there are certain [people] out there that would love to see me get killed, but that's a part of my life. When the cops told me they have information from valid sources that there is a hit out on my life, I say, "Tell me something I don't know."[77]

Because of his early boxing experience, 50 Cent enjoys the friendship of boxers like Mike Tyson and attending fights.

Threats and Enemies

Drug dealers are considered one source of threats against 50 Cent. Police still do not know who hired a gunman to kill 50 Cent in 2000. However, police at the time speculated that it could have been one of the drug dealers in the New York area who were angry that 50 Cent mentioned them in his song "Ghetto Qu'ran (Forgive Me)."

Another group of people who might want to harm 50 Cent are fellow rappers like Ja Rule (Jeffrey Atkins) who have feuded with the star for several years. The bad feelings between 50 Cent and Ja have exploded into violence several times. 50 Cent and Ja fought each other in 1999 when they attended a party in Atlanta, Georgia. Ja was upset about negative comments 50 Cent was making about him in records, and he started the fight by pulling 50 Cent's shirt over his head and hitting him in the stomach. 50 Cent then punched him in the eye. A more serious incident occurred on March 24, 2000, at the Hit Factory, a Manhattan recording studio. 50 Cent was stabbed in the chest during a fight with Ja and several of his friends. "I ended up getting three stitches. A nick ... it was a scratch," 50 Cent said.[78] The wound was minor, but he still had to go to the hospital for treatment.

50 Cent's beefs with rappers have also been linked to two shooting incidents. On September 10, 2003, someone fired at 50 Cent's limousine as it neared the Doubletree Hotel in Jersey City, New Jersey; neither 50 Cent nor anyone with him was hurt. A second shooting occurred on February 28, 2005, in the lobby of New York's Hot 97 radio station while 50 Cent was on the air declaring that West Coast rapper Game (Jayceon Terrell Taylor) was no longer a part of his G-Unit recording group. A member of 50 Cent's "posse," the friends, bodyguards, and employees he travels with, was wounded in the leg.

The rapper was also indirectly connected to a March 20, 2007, assault on the 14-year-old son of Jimmy "Henchmen" Rosemond, who manages Game. G-Unit member Tony Yayo allegedly slapped the youth as he was leaving his father's Czar Entertainment office in New York. 50 Cent denied any involvement in the incident.

Wearing a bulletproof vest is part of 50 Cent's daily routine.

Is 50 Cent Still a Thug?

The violence that surrounds 50 Cent makes some people believe he is still a criminal. He claims that the news media makes it seem like he is a criminal by repeating the charge in stories: "The misperception is gangster 50 [50 Cent]. That's the biggest misconception."[79] People who know 50 Cent disagree with the media's interpretation of his personality.

Terence Winter, who wrote the script for *Get Rich or Die Tryin*,' spent two months on tour with 50 Cent to research his life. Winter

50 Cent and Violence

Many people condemned advertising for the film *Get Rich or Die Tryin'* because it featured violent images such as 50 Cent pointing a gun. But 50 Cent said the images were justified because they represented the brutality of inner city life that the movie was trying to illustrate:

> You have people who are trying to capture what actually goes on in the environment, because the environment is violent. If we could just take the records of who goes in the hospital for one week in my neighborhood, you'll find far more victims of violent crimes, whether its stab wounds or gunshot wounds or whatever it is [than in many other neighborhoods]. It's what goes on in their environments and what they're writing about. And as far as the billboard is concerned, I feel like their standard [to condemn it] is based on music as an art form [but] I don't feel like they have a problem with [violent advertising] in film. If we go into our local Blockbuster, we're gonna see guns continuously throughout the whole place. We might even see more guns on covers than people's faces!

Lauren Saft, "An Interview with 50 Cent." Club Planet Archives, November 4, 2005. www.clubplanet.com/news/archive/the_50_cent_interview.asp.

Gaining Confidence

After completing the work on his second album, 50 Cent explained to *Vibe* magazine how he had gained more confidence as a recording artist. When asked if he felt that his album *The Massacre* would be just as good as his last, he replied:

"Absolutely, I think better. I did everything on my first album for the first time. This time, I'm a little more experienced. I know what to expect. I figured out that there's four things that it takes for you to be a celebrity or a star. That's quality in material, performance, appearance and personality. And I found my comfort zone.

Now, they're actually going to get to see more of me. In the beginning, you don't know exactly what to allow people to see and what you shouldn't allow them to see. And now I'm to the point to that it doesn't matter… I'm content with where I'm at. It's not even about finances at this point. It's more about what I want to do creatively."

Tanisha Blakely. "Online Exclusive: A Conversation With 50 Cent" [POSTED: March 4, 2005] http://www.vibe.com/news/online_exclusives/2005/03/online_exclusive_

was amazed to discover that 50 Cent was nice and not the wild and dangerous person some stories had described him as. "The thing that struck me more than anything," said Winter, "was how dull [being with 50 Cent] was. I guess I was expecting some sort of insanity and it just didn't happen."[80] Many other people who have worked with 50 Cent agree with Winter. Viola Davis played his grandmother in *Get Rich or Die Tryin'.* She said 50 Cent was always polite to her. "He's soft-spoken. Not egotistical," she said.[81]

That nice guy image can also be seen in 50 Cent's healthy lifestyle. Winter said 50 Cent got up every day at 7 A.M. to lift weights and work out to stay in shape. He was even more amazed that the rapper did not drink alcohol. 50 Cent does not consume alcohol or take drugs because of the way his uncles and aunts abused drugs when he was growing up: "I don't drink. I grew up around alcoholics. Why would I drink?"[82] 50 Cent also does charitable work. As a high school dropout himself, he started G-UNITY, a foundation that gives scholarships to poor students from his former high school so they can attend college.

Negative publicity

The many positive things about 50 Cent, however, are counter-balanced by negative incidents in his life. Although 50 Cent is considered a loving father, he has been criticized for allowing Marquise to appear on stage during concerts wearing a bullet-proof vest and swearing at the audience. 50 Cent has also had several minor brushes with the law. On New Year's Eve 2002, he and four other people were arrested and charged with weapons

50 Cent sometimes appears at concerts with his son, Marquise.

possession for having two loaded guns in their car. And 50 Cent almost went to jail for an incident on May 8, 2004, in Springfield, Massachusetts. When someone squirted water at 50 Cent while he was performing at a nightclub, he angrily jumped off the stage into the crowd. He was charged with punching one woman and kicking another. A judge spared him a jail sentence but ordered 50 Cent to do public service announcements against gun violence. He also ordered 50 Cent to pay medical expenses for the women and $3,000 in legal fees.

50 Cent and the News Media

Like other celebrities, 50 Cent hates the news media for running negative stories about him. He said stories that appeared after he was arrested on New Year's Eve 2002 for having guns in his car is an example of that:

> That incident got me back in the papers again: RAPPER 50 CENT ARRESTED WITH GUNS. Every time I was in the newspaper, it was for some [incident] that didn't have anything to do with music. They had my picture in the paper next to some notorious heavyweights [criminals] from the Queens drug game. That left a negative impression on people, since the things the paper said about me were never positive. And because the lyrical content of my records reflects the environment that I'm from, it all came together in people's minds: *50 Cent is a problem.* I'll be honest, I loved the free publicity. But controversy doesn't sell records—it just gets attention. Once I had the attention, I had to make sure the music could live up to the hype.

50 Cent with Kris Ex, *From Pieces to Weight: Once Upon A Time in Southside Queens.* New York: MTV Books, 2005, p. 216.

50 Cent the Gangsta'

Although 50 Cent cannot carry a gun because he is a convicted criminal, he wears a Gucci shoulder holster as a fashion accessory. The empty holster is simply part of 50 Cent's "gangsta' rapper" stage persona, which he believes he needs to maintain in order to remain popular. 50 Cent once explained how important it was for him to continue to appeal to young inner city blacks:

> That's my core base, so if that's gone I don't think I'll exist long. It might be one day [his fans] decide, "Oh 50's not hot no more, this other guy is," and I'm gone. If your original base is not there, how do you expect to stay?[83]

To keep his fans, 50 Cent continues to write songs that are filled with violent images, have criminals as heroes, and praise drug use and uninhibited sex. Many people consider these themes to be offensive and are also upset at lyrics that deride gay people—50 Cent has admitted publicly that he hates homosexuals—and refer to women as "ho's" (whores). Rappers have always been criticized for content of this kind, but even people who like rap have begun attacking it. In February 2007, disc jockey Orlando Davis of hip-hop station WLLD-FM in St. Petersburg, Florida, said "Gangsta rap has been destructive as the [Ku Klux] Klan to black culture. [It's] like a cancer, or like crack going into the neighborhoods."[84] His comments came at a panel discussion on rap.

However, 50 Cent defends gangsta' rap. He claimed in May 2007 that the music is a genuine interpretation of life in black inner cities and that rappers only give fans what they want to hear: "Music is a mirror and hip-hop is a reflection of the environment we grew up in, the harsh realities. [It's] difficult to find hip-hop that has had any success that hasn't had content on some level that was a little racy."[85]

Spreading Violence

Critics claim that violent messages in many songs are the worst part about rap because they can lead to real violence. This concern spilled over into advertising for the movie *Get Rich or*

Die Tryin' because billboards showed 50 Cent holding a microphone in one hand and a gun in the other. After protests, the advertisements were removed in Los Angeles, Philadelphia, and some cities in England. Lucy Cope, founder of Mothers Against Guns, argued that the movie's image glamorized guns. The billboard was dramatic because of 50 Cent's past, but Cope said, "My son died of one bullet. 50 cent is very lucky to be shot nine times and survived."[86] 50 Cent defended himself by claiming that he did not choose the image for the billboard.

The belief that songs, films, and posters that dramatize violence can also lead to violence came true when *Get Rich or Die Tryin'* was released. Shelton Flowers, 30, was shot to death on November 11, 2005, when the film opened at Loews Waterfront Movie Theater in West Homestead, Pennsylvania. He was killed in an argument with three other men. The shooting caused some theaters to stop showing the movie.

50 Cent issued a statement in which he said, "I feel for the victim's family in this situation."[87] Generally, however, 50 Cent has not apologized for his gangster image or any negative things he has done. In fact, the rapper believes he deserves a lot of credit for having achieved so much considering his background. In *From Pieces to Weight*, he wrote:

> I don't consider myself a role model, because I think a role model should be speaking and saying something positive all the time. That ain't me. But my story has to be an inspiration to people that's from the bottom, people that's from the same walks of life I'm from. I'm proof that success is possible. They can look at me and say, 'I know I could do this, because he did that.'[88]

Tryin' to Get Richer

With an attitude like that, 50 Cent is not going to quit doing what he thinks he must do to achieve success. And the restless ambition to become rich that first drove 50 Cent to sell drugs as a teenager was still alive after he had made millions of dollars.

In fact, he said his ambition was strengthened when he bought Tyson's home because it became a constant reminder that he could be poor again (Tyson had to sell his home because he was broke):

> When I wake up in the morning, when I'm at home, I wake up in a house where the man who owned it before me earned $500 million in his career and he doesn't have that money anymore. It reminds me that I have to be conscious of everything that I'm doing, regardless of how successful I become.[89]

Tyson wasted almost his entire fortune on lavish spending and poor money management. 50 Cent vows that will never happen to him and that he will keep working hard to get even richer before he dies.

Introduction: Worth a Lot More Than "Fifty Cents"

1. Roger Ebert, "Rapper 50 Cent impresses in film debut based on his life." *The Denver Post*, November 9, 2005, p. F9.
2. 50 Cent with Kris Ex, *From Pieces to Weight: Once Upon A Time in Southside Queens*. New York: MTV Books, 2005, p. 218.
3. Quoted in Jake Brown, *50 Cent: No Holds Barred*. Phoenix. AZ: Colossus Books, 2005, p. 3.
4. Quoted in Todd Hill, "The Man Behind the '50 Cent Persona' Speaks Out." *Staten Island Advance*, November 8, 2005. p. 1
5. Quoted in Chris Strauss, "Banking On 50 CENT." *People*, November 21, 2005, p. 39.

Chapter 1: Growing Up Poor, Black, and an Orphan

6. Quoted in Geoff Boucher, "A rapper learns how to cry; Laughter is easy. But it's rough, emotional and ugly as 50 Cent relives his traumas for the screen." *Los Angeles Times*, June 19, 2005, p. E1.
7. Quoted in Toure, "The Life of A Hunted Man." *Rolling Stone*, April 3, 2003, p. 46.
8. Quoted in Brown, *50 Cent: No Holds Barred*, p. 1.
9. Quoted in Paul Russell. Real Detroit interviews 50 Cent. February 8, 2003. www.rapnewsdirect.com/Interviews/0-202-1452-00.html.
10. Quoted in John K. Wiley, "50 Cent wins over director; Winkler expands rapper's role in new action movie." *Columbian*, May 9, 2006, p. D3.
11. 50 Cent, *From Pieces to Weight*, p. 29.
12. 50 Cent, *From Pieces to Weight*, p. 82.
13. Quoted in Brown, *50 Cent: No Holds Barred*, p. 18.
14. Quoted in Toure, "The Life of A Hunted Man." *Rolling Stone*, April 3, 2003, p. 48.

Chapter 2: Curtis Jackson Becomes 50 Cent

15. 50 Cent, *From Pieces to Weight*, p. 161.
16. Quoted in Josh Tyrangiel, "Rap's Newest Target." *Time*, February 17, 2003, p. 68.
17. Ethan Brown, *Queens Reigns Supreme: Fat Cat, 50 Cent, and the Rise of the Hip-Hop Hustler*. New York: Anchor Books, 2005, p. xxi.
18. Quoted in Mark Binelli, "No. 1 With a Bullet." *Rolling Stone*, February 6, 2003, p. 31.
19. 50 Cent, *From Pieces to Weight*, p. 165.
20. Quoted in Brown, *Queens Reigns Supreme*, p. 142.
21. Quoted in Brown, *50 Cent*, p. 33.
22. Quoted in Mark Binelli, "No. 1 With a Bullet." *Rolling Stone*, February 6, 2003, p. 31.
23. 50 Cent, *From Pieces to Weight*, p. 182.
24. Quoted in Davey D. Interview with 50 Cent January 8, 2003. Davey D's Hip Hop Corner. www.daveyd.com/interview50cent.html.
25. Quoted in Toure, "The Life of A Hunted Man." *Rolling Stone*, April 3, 2003, p. 46.
26. 50 Cent, *From Pieces to Weight*, p. 190.
27. Quoted in Allison Samuels, "50 CENT: Q&A." *Newsweek*, Feruary 17, 2003, p. 43.
28. Quoted in Craig Semon, "50 Cent and his ego lead to 'The Massacre.'" *Telegram & Gazette*, March 27, 2005, p. G5.
29. Quoted in Chris Strauss, "Banking On 50 CENT." *People*, November 21, 2005, p. 39.

Chapter 3: 50 Cent Becomes a Rap Superstar

30. Quoted in Toure, "The Life of A Hunted Man." *Rolling Stone*, April 3, 2003, p. 46.
31. 50 Cent, "Tupac Shakur: The Immortals." *Rolling Stone*, April 21, 2005, p. 94.
32. 50 Cent, *From Pieces to Weight*, p. 196.
33. Quoted in Brown, *50 Cent*, p. 163.
34. Quoted in Toure, "The Life of A Hunted Man." *Rolling Stone*, April 3, 2003, p. 48.

35. Quoted in Shaheem Reed and Sway Calloway, "50 Cent: Money to Burn." www.mtv.com/bands/123/50_Cent/news_feature_021203/.

36. Quoted in Allison Samuels, "50 CENT: Q&A." *Newsweek*, February 17, 2003, p. 43.

37. Quoted in Davey D. Interview with 50 Cent January 8, 2003. Davey D's Hip Hop Corner. www.daveyd.com/interview50cent.html.

38. Kelefa Sannch, "Music: The Highs; The Albums and Songs of the Year." *The New York Times*, December 28, 2003, p. AR31.

39. Quoted in Toure, "The Life of A Hunted Man." *Rolling Stone*, April 3, 2003, p. 48.

40. Quoted in Davey D. Interview with 50 Cent January 8, 2003. Davey D's Hip Hop Corner. www.daveyd.com/interview50cent.html.

41. Quoted in Jeff Otto, "Interview: 50 Cent." September 6, 2005. IGN (Imagine Games Network) movies.ign.com/articles/647/647683p1.html.

Chapter 4: The Ultimate Gangster Rapper

42. Quoted in Steve Jones, "Carrying on the gangsta mystique, trends come and go, but thug life endures." *USA Today*, May 23, 2003, p. E1.

43. Quoted in Brown, *Queens Reigns Supreme*, p. 186.

44. Quoted in Toure, "The Life of A Hunted Man." *Rolling Stone*, April 3, 2003, p. 45.

45. Quoted in Sannch, "Music: The Highs; The Albums and Songs of the Year," p. AR31.

46. Quoted in Chris Riemenschneider, "No. 1 WITH A BULLET; 50 Cent leads a revival of gangsta rap's violent images, high lifestyle and bitter feuds." *Star Tribune* (Minneapolis, Minn.) July 13, 2003, p. F1.

47. Quoted in Josh Tyrangiel, "Rap's Newest Target." *Time*, February 9, 2003. www.time.com/time/magazine/article/0,9171,421035,00.html.

48. Quoted in Toure, "The Life of A Hunted Man." *Rolling Stone*, April 3, 2003, p. 45.

49. Quoted in Jim DeRogatis, "Small change; 50 Cent is all street but lacks musical cred." *Chicago Sun-Times*, April 4, 2003, p. N5.
50. Quoted in Gail Mitchell, "Can 50 Cent Do It Again?" *Billboard*, February 26, 2005, p. 20.
51. Quoted in Brown, *Queens Reigns Supreme*, p. 203.
52. Quoted in Allison Samuels, "The Flip Side of 50 CENT." *Newsweek*, February, 21, 2005, p. 56.

Chapter 5: 50 Cent the Rapper Businessman

53. Quoted in Onsiri Pravattiyagul, "The Road to Riches." *The Bangkok (Thailand) Post*, March 11, 2006. p. 1.
54. Quoted in Jeff Otto, "Interview: 50 Cent." September 6, 2005. IGN (Imagine Games Network) movies.ign.com/articles/647/647683p1.html.
55. Quoted in Larry Fine, "Gangsta rapper's debut is 75 percent factual." *Seattle Times*, November 8, 2005, p. E4.
56. Quoted in Roger Ebert, "Rapper 50 Cent impresses in film debut based on his life." *The Denver Post*, November 9, 2005, p. F9.
57. Quoted in John K. Wiley, "Rapper lends street savvy to role in Iraq war picture." *Journal–Gazette* (Fort Wayne, Indiana), May 26, 2006, p. W6.
58. Quoted in Lauren Saft, Interview with 50 Cent November 4, 2005. Clubplanet Archives. www.clubplanet.com/news/archive/the_50_cent_interview.asp.
59. Quoted in Allison Samuels, "The Flip Side of 50 CENT." *Newsweek*, February, 21, 2005, p. 56.
60. Quoted in Brown, *50 Cent*, p. 155.
61. Quoted in "Credo: 50 Cent." *The Independent & The Independent on Sunday* (London, England). news.independent.co.uk/people/profiles/article2494170.ece.
62. Quoted in Onsiri Pravattiyagul, "The Road to Riches." *The Bangkok (Thailand) Post*, March 11, 2006, p. 1.
63. Quoted in Nathan Burstein, "Gunshots and thuggery end in 'shalom'." *Jerusalem (Israel) Post*, June 19, 2006, p. 24.
64. Quoted in Dmytro Zezyulin, "50 Cent brings his rap music to Ukraine." *Ukrainian Weekly* (Jersey City, New Jersey), June 11, 2006, p. 3.

65. Quoted in Gail Mitchell, "Can 50 Cent Do It Again?" *Billboard*, February 26, 2005, p. 21.
66. Quoted in Ray Waddell, "50 Brings Hip-Hop To The Speedway." *Billboard*, June 26, 2004, p. 18.
67. Quoted in Allison Samuels, "The Flip Side of 50 CENT." *Newsweek*, February, 21, 2005, p. 56.
68. 50 Cent and Noire, *Baby Brother*. New York: G–Unit Books, 2007, p. 1.
69. Quote in Marc Saltzman, "Fifty comes out blazin." *National Post* (Don Mills, Ontario), July 27, 2005, p. AL4.
70. Quoted in Neil Drumming, "50 + CHANGE." *Entertainment Weekly*, November 11, 2005, p. 26.

Chapter 6: A 50 Cent Lifestyle

71. Quoted in Shaheem Reed and Sway Calloway, "50 Cent: Money to Burn." www.mtv.com/bands/123/50_Cent/news_feature_021203/.
72. Quoted in Lauren Saft, "An Interview with 50 Cent." Club Planet Archives, November 4, 2005. www.clubplanet.com/news/archive/the_50_cent_interview.asp.
73. Quoted in Allison Samuels, "The Flip Side of 50 CENT." *Newsweek*, February, 21, 2005, p. 56.
74. Quoted in Evan Serpick, "Shooting 50 Cent." *Rolling Stone*, May 18, 2006, p. 211.
75. Quoted in Paul Russell. Real Detroit interviews 50 Cent. February 8, 2003. www.rapnewsdirect.com/Interviews/0-202-1452-00.html.
76. Quoted in Brown, *50 Cent*, p. 144.
77. Quoted in Erik Parker, "50 cent connection." *Rolling Stone*, December 12, 2002, p. 18.
78. Quoted in Brown, *50 Cent*, p. 100.
79. Quoted in Jeff Otto, "Interview: 50 Cent." September 6, 2005. IGN (Imagine Games Network) movies.ign.com/articles/647/647683p1.html.
80. Quoted in Todd Hill, "The Man Behind the '50 Cent Persona' Speaks Out." *Staten Island Advance*, November 8, 2005. p. 1.
81. Quoted in Chris Strauss, "Banking On 50 CENT." *People*, November 21, 2005, p. 39.

82. Quoted in Allison Samuels, "The Flip Side of 50 CENT." *Newsweek*, February, 21, 2005, p. 56.

83. Quoted in Shaheem Reed and Sway Calloway, "50 Cent: Money to Burn." www.mtv.com/bands/123/50_Cent/news_feature_021203/.

84. Quoted in Eric Deggans, "Words Can Hurt." *St. Petersburg (Florida) Times*, February 20, 2007, p. E1.

85. Quoted in Gail Mitchell, "50 Cent, T.I. Speak Their Minds On Lyric Censorship." May 17, 2007. www.billboard.com/bbcom/news/article_display.jsp?vnu_content_id=1003586995.

86. Quoted in Talise D. Moorer, "Protesting "Get Rich." *New York Amsterdam News*, November 10, 2005, p. 1.

87. Quoted in "A Shooting shocks rapper." *The Ottawa [Ontario, Canada] Citizen*. November 12, 2005, p. F8.

88. 50 Cent with Kris Ex, *From Pieces to Weight: Once Upon A Time in Southside Queens*. New York: MTV Books, 2005, p. 218.

89. Quoted in Todd Hill, "The Man Behind the '50 Cent Persona' Speaks Out." *Staten Island Advance*, November 8, 2005. p. 1.

1975

Curtis James Jackson III is born in Queens, New York, on July 6, 1975.

1994

50 Cent is arrested on felony drug charges on June 29 for selling cocaine to an undercover New York police officer. On July 19 he is arrested after police find heroin and crack cocaine, drug packaging material, and a starter gun at his grandmother's home. He is sentenced to seven months in a youth "shock incarceration" boot camp.

1997

50 Cent's son Marquise Jackson is born.

1999

50 Cent signs with Columbia Records.

2000

On May 24, 50 Cent is shot nine times in New York City. Columbia subsequently drops plan to release this debut album.

2001

50 Cent's parole term on 1994 drug charges comes to an end in January.

2002

Guess Who's Back mix-tape is released on May 21. 50 Cent is signed by Shady/Aftermath Records in June. In October, 50 Cent sings on the *8 Mile* movie soundtrack with the tracks "Wanksta," "Love Me," and "Places To Go."

2003

50 Cent releases his debut album, *Get Rich or Die Tryin'* on February 6.

2005

50 Cent releases the album *The Massacre* on March 3. The song's first single, "Candy Shop," becomes a massive hit. On August 9 50 Cent's autobiography—*From Pieces to Weight: Once Upon A Time in Southside Queens*—is published. On November 8 the soundtrack for the movie "Get Rich or Die Tryin'," is released and on November 11, the movie *Get Rich or Die Tryin'* opens in theaters. Shelton Flowers, 30, is shot to death at a theater in West Homestead, Pennsylvania, after a showing of the movie.

2007

50 Cent's third album, *Curtis*, is released on June 27.

Books

50 Cent with Noah Callahan-Bever, *50 X 50: 50 Cent in His Own Words*. New York: Pocket, 2007.

Hal Marcovitz, *50 Cent (Hip Hop)*. Broomall, Pennsylvania: Mason Crest Publishers, 2006.

Mary Boone, 50 Cent (*Blue Banner Biographies*). Hockessin, Delaware: Mitchell Lane Publishers (September 15, 2006).

Internet Sources

50 Cent Official Site (www.50cent.com). This site includes information about 50 Cent from various media sources, a biography, videos, photographs, and links to sites related to the rapper.

50 Cent (www.mtv.com/music/artist/50_cent/artist.jh). This MTV site has news, tour dates, video, and audio of 50 Cent's music.

50 Cent: Artist Main (www.vh1.com/artists/az/50_cent/artist.jhtml). This VH1 site has information on 50 Cent's albums and concerts, news, a biography, and message boards about the rapper.

All Hip Hop (www.allhiphop.com). The site contains the latest daily news on 50 Cent and other rappers as well as photos, downloads, and many other features.

Davey D's Hip-Hop Corner: The New Source For The Hip-Hop Generation (www.daveyd.com). The official site of hip-hop journalist Davey D contains music, news, and other material on rappers like 50 Cent.

G-Unit World (www.gunitworld.com). The site contains facts, photos, videos, musical downloads, and other material about 50 Cent and other G-Unit rappers as well as G-Unit merchandise.

Michael V. Uschan has written more than fifty books including *Life of An American Soldier in Iraq*, for which he won the 2005 Council for Wisconsin Writers Juvenile Nonfiction Award. It was the second time he won the award. Mr. Uschan began his career as a writer and editor with United Press International, a wire service that provided stories to newspapers, radio, and television. Journalism is sometimes called "history in a hurry." Mr. Uschan considers writing history books a natural extension of the skills he developed in his many years as a journalist. He and his wife, Barbara, reside in the Milwaukee suburb of Franklin, Wisconsin.